THE MATHEMATICAL FUNFAIR

Brian Bolt

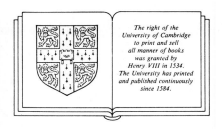

The right of the University of Cambridge to print and sell all manner of books was granted by Henry VIII in 1534. The University has printed and published continuously since 1584.

CAMBRIDGE UNIVERSITY PRESS

Cambridge
New York   Port Chester
Melbourne   Sydney

Published by the Press Syndicate of the University of Cambridge
The Pitt Building, Trumpington Street, Cambridge CB2 1RP
40 West 20th Street, New York, NY 10011, USA
10 Stamford Road, Oakleigh, Melbourne 3166, Australia

First published 1989
Reprinted 1990

Printed in Great Britain by Scotprint, Musselburgh, Scotland

British Library Cataloguing in Publication Data
Bolt, Brian
The mathematical funfair.
1. Mathematical puzzles
I. Title
793,7′4

ISBN 0 521 37743 9

CONTENTS

Page numbers in bold refer to the puzzles;
the second page number to the commentary.

Introduction

Mathematical puzzles and games appeal to a wide range of people from all walks of life. Puzzles appear in all sorts of places: on matchboxes, in Xmas crackers, on breakfast cereal packets, on beer mats, in newspapers, in magazines, and last but not least, in puzzle books. This book has been written following the success of my earlier book, *The Amazing Mathematical Amusement Arcade*. It has well over a hundred different puzzles with which to capture your imagination. They range widely from matchstick and coin puzzles, to railway shunting problems, number puzzles, chess-board puzzles, topological impossibilities, tricks, games, and yet more on magic squares. Some puzzles are variations on well tried but worth repeating themes, but there are enough original ones here to challenge the most ardent puzzler.

The second part of the book is given over to a detailed commentary so that you can check your solution, or find help when baffled. But don't give up too quickly for the real satisfaction comes in solving a puzzle for yourself.

Brian Bolt

1 Matchstick magic

Remove only four matches from the 3 × 3 array to leave exactly five identical squares.

What is the smallest number of matches you can remove to leave just two squares?

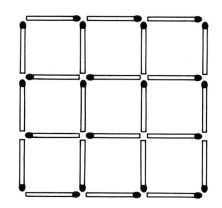

2 The car jam

In a small underground private car park in the centre of London the cars were packed in like sardines. So tightly were the cars parked that the only way a car could be moved was to push it forwards or backwards along its length. The car marked 1 in the diagram belonged to the managing director of the firm owning the car park. He was in a hurry to get out! Help the car park attendant by finding the minimum number of car moves required for car 1 to be released from the jam it is in.

A set of dominoes makes a very handy visual aid when trying to solve this puzzle.

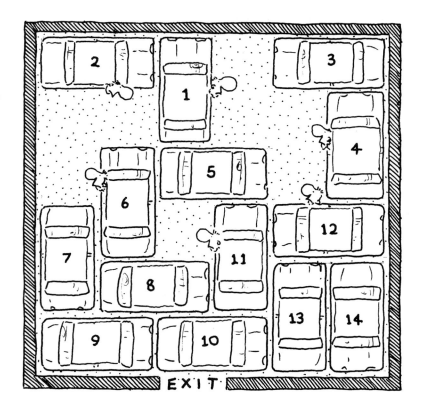

1

3   Who nobbled the racehorse?

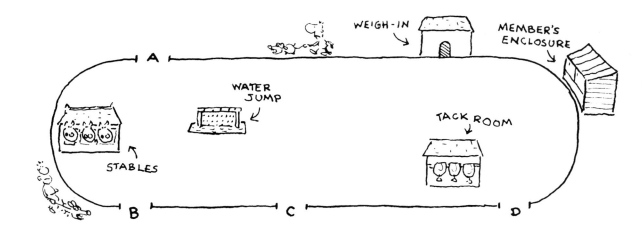

The favourite for the Winter Race Meeting at Aincot was stabled inside the racecourse on the night before the big race. Security inside the racecourse on that night was very tight with no one allowed inside the boundary fence from 11 p.m. until 7 a.m. the next morning. The guards and their dogs had had a cold night patrolling the grounds and at 7 a.m. when the four main gates were unlocked by the groundsmen and they were about to go home it began to snow. The snow delayed the arrival of the stable lad who entered at *B* and, before going to the stables to feed and exercise the favourite, had a few words in the tack room with the groom, who was there cleaning the saddle. He stayed with the horse right up to the start of the race, so imagine his distress when the horse ran very badly, finished last, and was shown to have been doped. He had his suspicions that one of the team of people surrounding the horse was guilty, so he set out to gather evidence about their movements between 7 a.m. and 7.15 a.m. when he had reached the stable. In this period of time he found that the owner of the horse had entered at *C* and strolled across to the member's enclosure. On the way the owner passed the trainer, who had entered at *D*, inspecting the water jump. The owner also saw the jockey on his way from *B* to the weigh-in, while the jockey passed the time of day with the groom, who had entered at *A*, when he was on his way to the tack room. They had all discussed the snow and remarked on their trails of footmarks which strangely didn't cross anywhere.

Who nobbled the horse?

4 The car importer

A new assignment of Japanese cars had just been off-loaded from the freighter onto the dockside. The car importer checked that they were all of the same model as ordered, and went to complete the necessary paper work with the customs officials. While there, he was intrigued to notice that the total retail value of all the new cars was £1 111 111.

What was the retail price of the car (a whole number of pounds) and how many were there?

5 Number pyramids

In the number pyramids which follow the numbers in each new level of the pyramid are derived from the level below by the simple addition rule shown on the right. Find the missing numbers in each case.

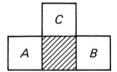

$C = A + B$

(a)

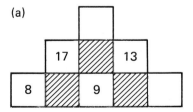

(b)

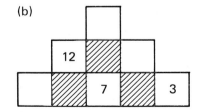

(c)

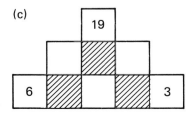

(d)

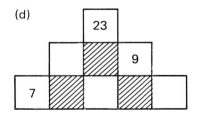

6 The triangular building site

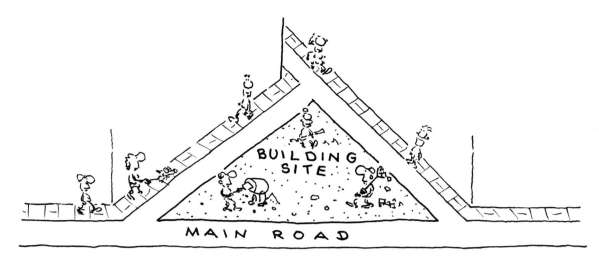

A builder acquired planning permission to erect three detached houses on a triangular building plot bounded by three roads. To make the best of the site the builder proposed to divide it into three triangular sites each having the same area.

How can this be done?

7 Ring the triangle

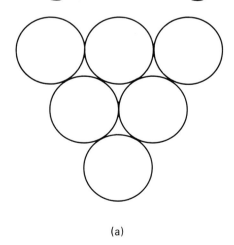

(a)

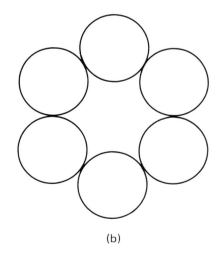

(b)

Make a triangle of six pennies as shown in (a). What is the smallest number of pennies you can move by sliding to form the ring of pennies as in (b), if every time a penny is moved it must be put into contact with two other pennies? Note you are not allowed to push one coin with another.

8 The jeweller's chain

A jeweller had an urgent order to make a chain with 25 links for a local mayor. At the time she had an assistant and five apprentices so they each set to with a will to make a part of the chain. The links were large so the jeweller was well pleased when by 5 o'clock they had made the 25 links. She then realised how inefficient they had been, for between them they had seven pieces of chain; two with 2 links, two with 3 links and one each of 4 links, 5 links and 6 links. To join the pieces into one chain of 25 links she would need to cut and rejoin some of the links. She reckoned that to cut and join a single link would take her 20 minutes so she decided to stay on and finish the job by herself.

What was the earliest time the jeweller could have gone home with the 25-link chain complete?

5

9 The anti-litter campaign

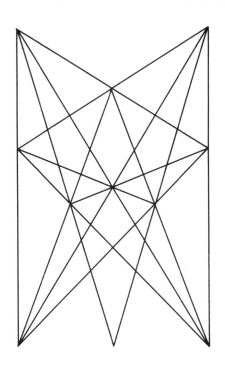

The city councillors were becoming very concerned about the amount of litter being left in their very beautiful park. To combat this they decided to instal a number of litter bins as strategically as possible. The park was criss-crossed in an intricate way by fourteen straight paths, as shown in the plan on the right, and the city fathers recommended that there should be a minimum of 3 litter bins on each path. The city treasurer protested at the likely cost, for he supposed it would require $14 \times 3 = 42$ bins, so he was pleasantly surprised when the park keeper showed him that the requirement could be met with far fewer bins.

What is the smallest number of bins required, and where should they be placed?

How many park attendants would be required to ensure that there is one on every path?

10 The railcar terminus

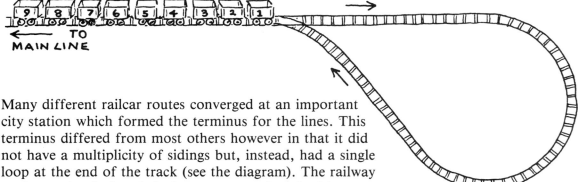

Many different railcar routes converged at an important city station which formed the terminus for the lines. This terminus differed from most others however in that it did not have a multiplicity of sidings but, instead, had a single loop at the end of the track (see the diagram). The railway engineer who designed the layout was praised for his economic use of land and the ingenious way in which the loop allowed the order of the railcars arriving at the station to be permuted for different departure patterns. Show how to use the loop to change the order of nine railcars which arrive in the order 1, 2, 3, 4, 5, 6, 7, 8, 9, so that they can depart in the order 7, 9, 8, 1, 2, 4, 5, 3, 6. Note that the loop is long enough to contain all the railcars together, if necessary, and that the railcars can travel around the loop in a clockwise direction.

11 Paving the patio

A keen gardener planned a new patio, in the form of a square, using 64 paving slabs. To add interest, he used an equal number of paving slabs in each of four colours. After much experimenting he ended up with a design which consisted of four identical interlocking shapes, one in each colour.

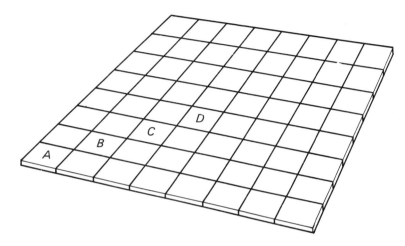

Each of the paving slabs labelled *A, B, C* and *D* in the diagram was a different colour. What was the design?

12 Mind stretching

We have all seen a glove or sock turned inside out, and it doesn't need much imagination to see that a ball with a hole cut in it could be turned inside out.

Imagine, however, an inner tube of a bicycle or lorry and imagine cutting a large hole where the valve would be.

By stretching the tube would it be possible to turn it inside out?

It may help you in your deliberations to make a model of the tube, when the hole has been stretched so that there is almost more hole than tube, using two strips of paper coloured to indicate the inside.

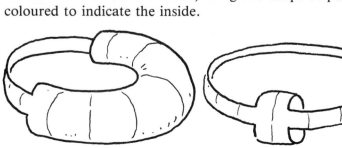

13 The chapel hymnboard

The Methodist chapel at the village of Trepolpen
prided itself on its singing and everything was
done to ensure that it kept its good reputation.
At each service the organist's wife carefully
placed the number cards in the hymnboard so
that all the congregation could clearly see which
hymn was to be sung next.

But after many years' use the cards had
become very worn and a disgrace. The last straw
came at the Harvest Festival service when there
were not enough serviceable numbers left to
display the hymns chosen by the visiting minister,
and the organist threatened to resign.

The result was an emergency meeting of the
chapel trustees at which they agreed that they
would order a new set of cards. At first they
estimated that with 15 positions for numbers on
the board and 10 different digits possible they
would require 150 cards, which they couldn't
afford. However, the organist's wife pointed out
that in her experience a 6 could double as a 9
when placed upside down, and that different
numbers could be put on the two sides of a card.
She felt sure she could design a set of cards so
that five of the 984 hymns in the Methodist
hymnbook could be put up on the board with
less than 100 cards.

What is the smallest number of cards which
would fulfil all the requirements?

14 One step forward, march!

Imagine 8 knights placed on
the black squares of a 4 × 4
board as shown. Show that
they can all manage to make
one move.

This is not difficult, but
the equivalent problem
starting with 13 knights on
the black squares of a 5 × 5
board is a different matter.
See what you can make of it!

15 Sim

This is a simple game for two players devised by Gustavus Simmons (hence its name).

Play starts with the six points A, B, C, D, E, F at the vertices of a hexagon inscribed in a circle. Players, using different coloured pencils or pens take turns to join a pair of the vertices with a straight line.

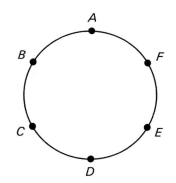

There are fifteen possible lines so the game must finish in a limited time, and the aim of the game is to avoid making a triangle of your colour, with vertices on the circle. If you do, you lose. Interestingly, it is not possible to draw all fifteen lines with two colours and avoid a triangle of one colour, so someone must lose!

The result of one game is shown here, with numbers to indicate the order in which the lines were drawn. The solid lines represent the first player P and the dotted lines the second player Q. It is Q's turn and the only possible moves are DF which completes DAF, and FE which completes EAF. So Q must lose.

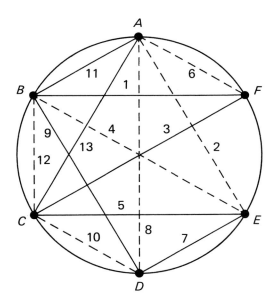

16 Complete the set

1   9   64   256   1296   2187   3125   4096

This series is incomplete. Spot the underlying pattern and supply the missing number.

17 The Old Girls' reunion

At their school's annual reunion five friends shared a table for dinner. Each friend ordered something to drink, a meat course and a dessert. Brenda and Mrs Burns had martinis while Betty and Mrs Brown ordered sherry. Ms Baker had a fruit juice since she was driving. Brenda and Miss Broad ordered steak. Beryl and Ms Baker had roast beef. For dessert Beryl and Miss Black ate gateau, while Barbara and Ms Baker had ice cream. The other friend had a fruit salad. No two friends sitting next to each other were served two things the same.

Who had duck and what did Bridget eat?

18 The chocolate manufacturer's dilemma

A manufacturer of chocolates designed a new box of chocolates to celebrate the firm's centenary. The box was carefully designed to just hold 48 identical spherical chocolates arranged in a single layer with 8 rows of 6.

Unfortunately, when all the preparations were complete it was found that the chocolates were 4% below their advertised weight. It was too late to redesign the boxes and too difficult to change the specification for the chocolates. But there is a neat way in which the manufacturer can overcome the dilemma. How?

19 The Ruby wedding

At their Ruby wedding celebrations William and Ruth had all their family to a party. Reflecting on their long life together William recalled how he had first fallen in love with 'young Ruth' when they had shared a desk at school together many years ago. Looking around at his children and their families he wondered whether they would all be together for a golden wedding anniversary and, so speculating, he realised that the difference between the square of his age and the square of his wife's age was exactly equal to the square of the number of their children.

How old were William and Ruth when they married, and how many children did they have?

20 The flight controller's nightmare

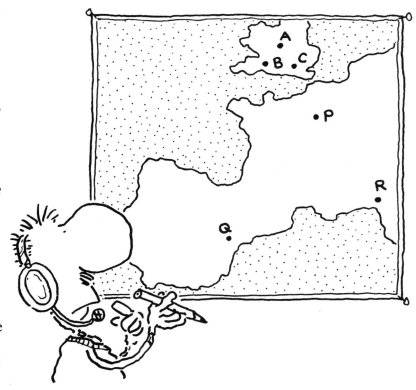

With the increase in package-holiday flights to the continent, a flight controller was responsible for trying to route safely an ever-increasing number of planes from the south of England to the continental resorts.

One particularly vexing problem was caused by three large companies who operated out of airports A, B and C respectively and who each wanted direct flights to the airports at P, Q and R. Because of the high density of traffic on these routes it was important that none of the flight paths should cross. Flying over an airport is quite out of the question. Can you find nine flight paths to solve the controller's problem?

21 Three of a kind

Find A, B and C to make the adjoining addition sum correct.

$$\begin{array}{r} A\,B\,C \\ +\ A\,B\,C \\ A\,B\,C \\ \hline B\,B\,B \end{array}$$

22 Coin contortions

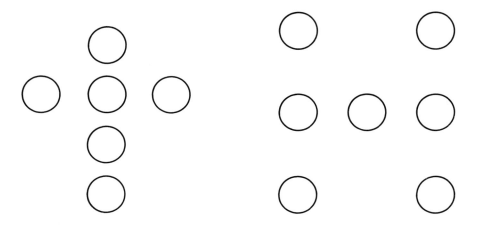

(*a*) Arrange six coins in the form of a cross as shown then move just one coin to form two lines with four coins in each line.

(*b*) Arrange seven coins in the form of an H as shown, then add two coins to form ten lines with three coins in each line.

23 An elephantine hole

A magician challenged his audience to cut a hole in a sheet of newspaper big enough for a fully grown elephant to walk through. No one took him up on it so he quickly demonstrated to them that it was a practical proposition which needed no sticky tape or magic shrinking potion for the elephant.

Can you do better than his audience?

24 Loading the ferry

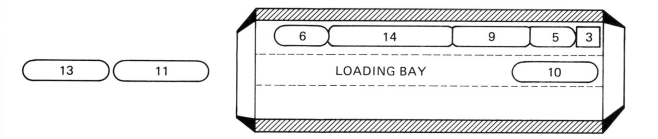

The only way to cross a wide river estuary was to use the ferry. The approach road to the ferry was very narrow so the traffic for the ferry had to queue in single file in the order in which it arrived. The ferry itself had a loading bay 40 metres long which could hold three lanes of traffic.

The person responsible for loading the ferry let the vehicles onto the ferry so that the left-hand lane was filled as far as possible before using the middle lane, and when the next vehicle in the queue was too long for the space left in the middle lane the vehicles were diverted to fill the right hand lane.

This strategy for loading the ferry meant that it was frequently loaded inefficiently, particularly when the queue contained several long lorries. The ferry owner became concerned about this for it was not only bad for public relations but significantly reduced his profits. To overcome the problem a device was installed which measured the length of each vehicle as it joined the ferry queue and fed the information into a computer which worked out the best lane of the ferry's loading bay for each vehicle. As each driver came to the head of the queue and drove up the loading ramp a green light came on over the appropriate lane.

On one occasion the lengths of the vehicles in the ferry queue, taken in order of arrival were

3 m, 5 m, 9 m, 14 m, 6 m, 10 m, 11 m,
13 m, 7 m, 8 m, 15 m, 11 m, 8 m, 4 m.

Before the computer was installed how many of these vehicles would have been loaded and what percentage of space would have been wasted?

Show that by carefully selecting the lane for each vehicle as it comes to the head of the queue it is possible to load the ferry to full capacity from this particular queue.

25 Postage due

At the end of the day a secretary was faced with putting
stamps on a large number of packages. She had plenty of
stamps but they were only in two denominations and she
was not sure that she would always be able to find the
right combination to match the postage due. However,
experience showed her that although she could not find a
combination of the stamps to make 39p, any higher
postage due could be arranged with a suitable combination
of the stamps available.

Assuming that the stamp denominations were a whole
number of pence, what were they?

26 Ann's tower

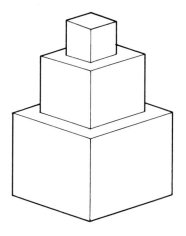
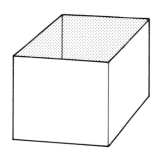

One of Ann's Christmas presents was a box of building
bricks. The bricks were all cubes with an edge of 5 cm and
completely filled the box which was also in the shape of a
cube. Like many young children Ann was fascinated with
building towers and it wasn't long before she had tipped
out all the bricks and started building. She started by
building a large cube, then a smaller cube on top of that
and a yet smaller cube on top of the latter. When the three
cubes were complete she could still look over the top of her
tower when standing, which disappointed her, but she had
the satisfaction that she had used every single brick in her
construction.
  How high was the tower?

27 Seeing is believing!

We are trained to interpret certain kinds of two-dimensional drawings as representing three-dimensional objects, and the ability to understand such diagrams and to draw them is an aid to thinking and communicating ideas about space. However, as the drawings illustrate, visual impossibilities can be created. Is the last drawing a 3-pin or a 2-pin plug? Can a staircase join up on itself? Could you make the triangle from three pieces of wood?

Visual perception is more the area of study of the psychologist than the mathematician, but diagrams are widely used by mathematicians to help in thinking about space so their shortcomings need to be recognised

The Dutch artist M C Escher made great play of creating impossible worlds based on the illusions in the drawings. See, for example, his lithographs entitled 'Waterfall', or 'Ascending and Descending', or 'House of Stairs', in *The Graphic Work of M.C. Escher*.

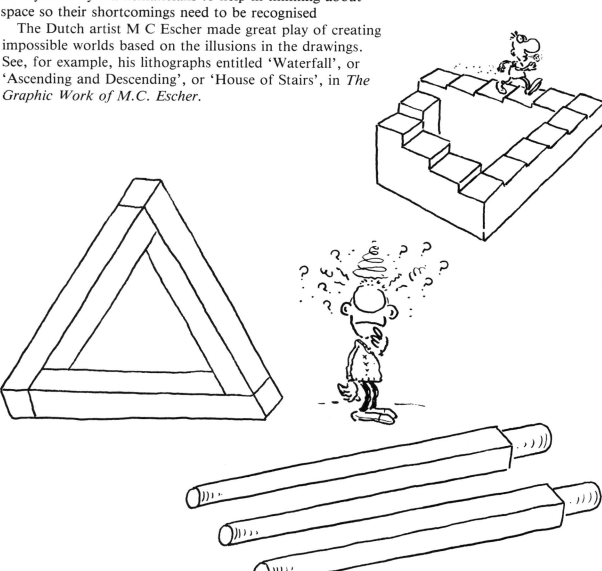

28 Reafforestation!

A part of the woodland owned by the forestry commission
needed thinning out. At the start there were 49 fir trees in
a 7×7 array as shown, but by the time the forestry
workers had done their job they had removed 29 trees and
managed to leave 20 trees so that they stood in 18 lines
with 4 trees in each!

How did they do it?

29 Find the route

It is possible to start at the top left hand corner, move one
square to a 1, then move two squares to a 2, then move
three squares to a 3, and so on, without revisiting any
square, and ending with the 8 in the bottom right hand
corner.

Moves can be made only vertically and horizontally not
diagonally.

See if you can find such a route.

Start	1	3	2	5	4	4	6
2	4	5	3	4	6	7	4
5	2	3	5	3	5	6	5
4	3	6	3	5	4	7	4
3	4	7	6	5	7	6	5
5	6	5	3	7	6	4	7
4	7	4	5	6	5	5	7
6	5	7	7	5	6	4	⑧

30 The tournament draw

For the end of season squash tournament there were 27 entries. The tournament was arranged on a knockout basis with the loser of each match being eliminated. A number of players received a bye in the first round so that from the second round onwards the number of players going forward at each stage was halved.

Norman and Theresa, the squash captains, met to arrange the draw. Their first problem was to decide how many matches would be needed in the first round and hence how many players should have byes. Norman was worried, he didn't really know how to begin, but Theresa with experience of organising tennis tournaments on similar lines was very quickly able to say how many rounds would be needed, how many byes to give and how many matches there would be in the whole tournament. What are the numbers involved?

How many matches would need to be played in a tournament with N players?

31 The police officer's beat

The map shows the streets which have to be patrolled by a police officer on the beat. The length of side of a small square represents 100 m, and the total length of road to be patrolled is 2.5 km. What is the shortest distance the police officer can walk to patrol the whole beat?

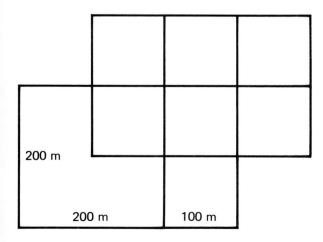

200 m

200 m   100 m

32 Gale

This is a game devised by David Gale who was a professor of mathematics at Brown University. The playing area consists of two rectangles of intermeshed dots. In the area shown the rectangles are both 6 × 5 and one set of dots is shown as crosses to make them distinguishable. Player *A* tries to make a continuous path between side *a* and side *a'* joining the crosses, while player *B* tries to make a continuous path between side *b* and side *b'* joining the dots.

Players take turns to join any pair of adjacent dots or crosses, with vertical or horizontal, but not diagonal, lines. Paths may not cross!

The board shows the end of a game won by *A*.

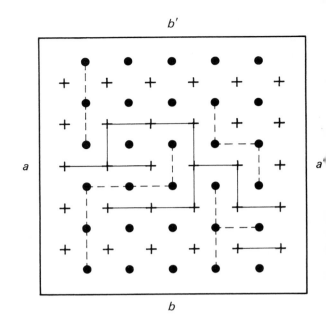

33 The stamp machine

A stamp machine was being designed so that in return for a 20p coin and a 10p coin it would eject a strip of stamps worth 30p. To gain publicity the Post Office decided to hold a competition. The public were asked to suggest the values for the individual stamps in a strip, so that any letter or package could be stamped correctly with sums from 1p to 30p.

In the end they awarded two first prizes of free postage for a year, one to Mrs Royale Mail and the other to the Rev Énue. Mrs Royale Mail had shown that the problem could be solved with a strip of just five stamps, and her solution was eventually used.

What were the values of the five stamps?

The Rev Énue, however, had found a solution where any of the values from 1p to 30p could be found by using a single stamp or a *connected* set of stamps. One way to do this would be to have a strip of thirty 1p stamps but you can do a lot better than that! What is the smallest number of stamps which could be used to achieve this, and what will be their values and order on the strip?

34 Billy Bunter's bargain

Billy Bunter was delighted when the manufacturer of
SCRUNCH, his favourite chocolate bar, decided to have a
special promotion for a limited period. They authorised the
shopkeepers to give a bar, free, to anyone presenting them
with eight SCRUNCH labels.

   Billy persuaded all his friends to donate their labels to him,
and by the end of the period he had collected 71 labels.

   How many free SCRUNCH bars was Billy able to collect
at his school tuckshop?

35 All touching

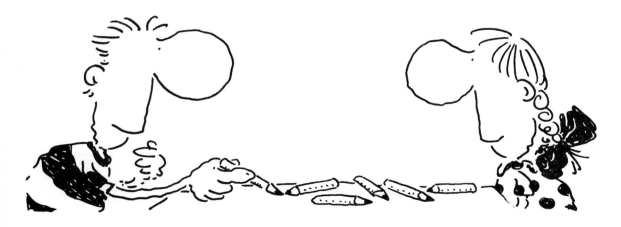

Show how to arrange six pencils (or matchsticks) so that each
of them is touching the other five.
Now show that seven pencils can be arranged so that they
all touch each other.

36   1984 revisited

This activity has nothing to do with George Orwell!
(a) Did you know that $1985^2 - 1984^2$ is a perfect square? When did this last happen?
(b) It is not very difficult to express 1984 using eight '4' digits and any mathematical symbols you might care to use, but it will tax your ingenuity to do the same using four '8' digits.

37   Identical twins, quads and triplets

What must 49 be multiplied by to produce 4949?

What must 38 be multiplied by to produce 383838?

Find four prime numbers whose product with any 2-digit number *ab* will turn it into the 6-digit number *ababab*.

Investigate the effect on 2-digit numbers of the product $73 \times 101 \times 137$.

38   Rhyme around

Sir, I bear a rhyme excelling
In mystic force and magic spelling
Celestial sprites elucidate
All my own striving can't relate.

See, I have a rhyme assisting
My feeble brain, its tasks ofttimes resisting.

Both these rhymes were composed for the same purpose.
What was that purpose?

39 Touching coins

(*a*) The first problem is to place four identical coins in such a way that they are all the same distance from each other. The solution is not a square array, as the diagram shows, for the distance from A to C is more than the distance from A to B. There is more than one solution, but the best has the centres of the coins equidistant from each other.

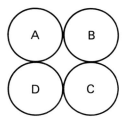

(*b*) It is easy to place four coins so that they each touch a fifth coin, but how can you place five identical coins so that they each touch all the others?

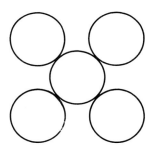

40 Two wrongs make a right

```
   W R O N G
 + W R O N G
   ‾‾‾‾‾‾‾‾‾
   R I  G H T
```

In spite of what we are always told two wrongs can make a right if each letter in the adjoining sum is taken to stand for a different digit.
Can you find a solution?

41 Narcissistic numbers

The number 153 has the interesting property that it is equal to the sum of the cubes of its digits.

$$1^3 + 5^3 + 3^3 = 1 + 125 + 27 = 153$$

370 is another number with the same property.

Ignoring unity, there are two further numbers, both less than 500 with the same property. Can you find them?

42 Inside and out

Given five hoops with radii 50 cm, 40 cm, 20 cm, 20 cm and 10 cm, show how to overlap them so that the shaded area inside the largest hoop (see the diagram) is equal to the total area of the shaded shapes inside the four smaller hoops.

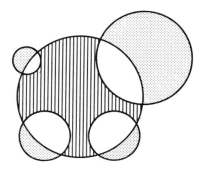

43 Matchstick manoeuvres

Move, not remove, four matches in the Os and Xs grid to form three identical squares.

There are three quite different solutions, can you find them?

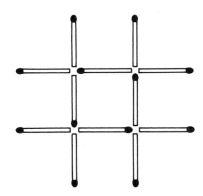

44 Micro millions

The micro millionaire studied his balance sheet at the end of the year with great interest. The total income from the sale of the very popular Domomicro model came to £1 000 000 000. What aroused his interest was not so much the total as that neither the number of micros sold nor the cost of an individual micro contained a single zero digit.

How many micros were sold?

45 The economy cut

Emma was always looking for ways to save money. While in the remnant shop she came across just the material she wanted to make a table-cloth.

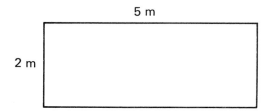

Unfortunately the piece of material was in the form of a 2 m × 5 m rectangle and her table was 3 m square. She bought it however having decided that the area was more than enough to cover the table. When she got home however she decided she had been a fool because she couldn't see how to cut up the material to make a square. But just as she despaired she had a brainwave, and with 3 straight cuts, in no time at all, she had 5 pieces which fitted neatly together in a symmetric pattern to form a square using all the material. How did she do it?

46 The variable menu

The owner of a transport cafe had many regular customers. So as not to bore them with a monotonous menu she devised a plan which would ensure that no two meals should repeat themselves for at least a year. She saw each meal as basically consisting of 4 parts (i) potatoes or equivalent, (ii) meat or fish (iii) a vegetable, (iv) a sweet. Her solution is embodied in the following table.

chips	pork	peas	apple pie
boiled potatoes	lamb	carrots	ice cream
roast potatoes	chicken	sweet corn	fruit salad
rice	fish	cabbage	
	beef	cauliflower	
		brussels sprouts	
		broad beans	

Starting on the first day of the year she served chips, pork, peas and apple pie and on each succeeding day she replaced each part of the meal by the next ingredient in the table. The next ingredient to the one at the bottom of a column being the one at the top so, for example, if on one day the meal was rice, fish, broad beans, and apple pie, on the next day it would be chips, beef, peas, and ice cream.

How many days pass before a meal repeats itself?

What meal is served on day 100 from the start of the scheme?

On what day would you expect to be served roast potatoes, lamb, brussels sprouts and apple pie?

The cafe became known for its variable menu and the trade increased so much that the owner appointed a new cook. Thinking to please the owner the new cook extended the table above by adding sausages to the meat column and turnips to the vegetable column. Why did the owner sack him?

47 Not in her prime

A computer programmer worked out the product of her age in years, the age of her cat in years, and the number of her house. Given that the product was 17 654 how old was she?

48 Loop-line limitations

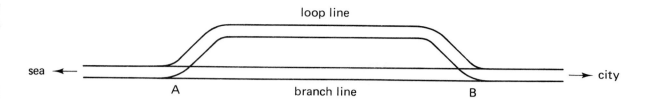

The branch line from the city main line station to a popular seaside resort only justified a single line because for most of the year the passenger traffic was light. This did create problems in the busy holiday period however so the railway company added a short loop line at the half-way point to allow trains to pass one another and thus enable trains to travel along the line in both directions at the same time. The loop line and the branch line between the points at A and B, see the diagram, could each take an engine and six carriages, or seven carriages.

This made passing easy as long as one of two trains meeting at this point could be wholly contained by the loop. Unfortunately on a busy Bank Holiday a relief station master allowed a train with 14 carriages to leave the seaside just as a train with 16 carriages left the city headed towards the sea. Many cross words were exchanged by the engine drivers when they met at the half-way point, but before they came to blows one of the passengers showed them an efficient way out of their dilemma. The passenger was a life-long puzzle freak and she saw the situation as an occasion to put her problem solving skills to practical use. She convinced the drivers that they could pass each other with a minimum of fuss – indeed one of the trains could stay coupled together for the whole of the operation. Show how the trains can pass with the minimum of stopping and starting by the engines.

49 As easy as abc!

Find numbers a, b and c such that

$$a^b \times c^a = abca$$

where $abca$ stands for a 4-digit number.

50 Magic polygons

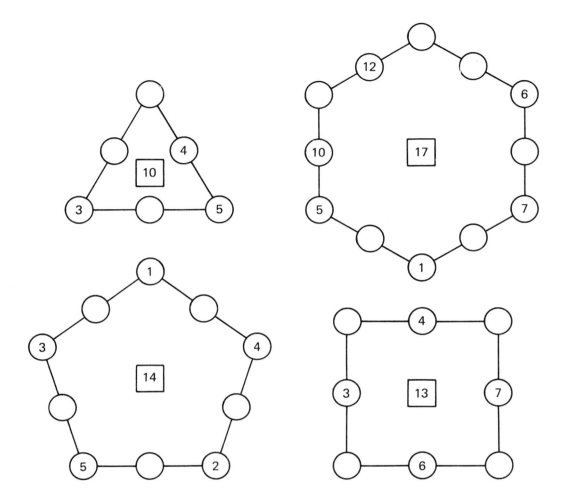

Complete these magic polygons by putting numbers in the circles so that the total along each side of the polygon is equal to the number given in the centre of each polygon. The numbers to be used for the triangle are 1 to 6, the numbers for the square 1 to 8, the numbers for the pentagon 1 to 10, and for the hexagon 1 to 12.

With the magic total given and many of the numbers already in place the solutions to the above polygons were relatively easy to find. The real problem is to try to find all the possible ways in which the same numbers could be put in the circles to make the polygons magic. The totals may not be the same, and there are at least four solutions in each case.

Investigate strategies for these polygons which could be used to search for solutions of polygons with more sides.

51 Factors galore

The number 3 785 942 160 made up of the ten digits 0, 1, 2, ...,
9 is divisible by all the integers from 1 to 18 inclusive. How
many other such numbers can you find?

52 Fascinating fractions

The digits 1, 2, 3, ..., 9 can be arranged to form two numbers
whose ratio is ½ as follows

$$\frac{7329}{14\,658} = \frac{1}{2}$$

This is interesting in itself, but even more fascinating is the
fact that the nine digits can also be arranged to form numbers
whose ratio is ⅓, ¼, ⅕, ⅙, ⅐, ⅛, ⅑.
   Get your calculator to work and see how many solutions
you can find.

53 How large a number can you make?

You can use the digits 1, 2 and 3 once only and any
mathematical symbols you are aware of, but no symbol is to
be used more than once. The challenge is to see who can
make the largest number. Here are some numbers to set the
ball rolling.

   321   21^3 $(3 \div .1)^2$

54 Food for thought

The row/column/diagonal total for a 3 × 3 magic square
is 20. The first two entries are given, what are the
remaining entries?

11	3	

55 How many will you take?

This is a game for two players. Start with a pile of counters (matchsticks, coins or paperclips will do).

Each player plays in turn and must remove either 1 or 2 or 3 counters from the pile. The player forced to remove the last counter loses the game.

Play the game with your friends and see if you can determine a winning strategy.

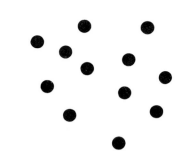

56 The dishonest gold exporter

Because gold is such a precious metal an exporter tried to make money by melting down the genuine gold ingots and recasting them in moulds which produced ingots which were one gram light. The customs officers became aware of this fraud from an undercover agent and set about trying to find the light ingots.

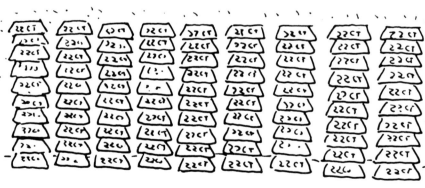

In their bonded warehouse at the time they had several consignments of 100 ingots each made up of 10 piles of 10 ingots. Their information told them that one pile of 10 ingots in each consignment came from the dishonest exporter and they wanted to find an efficient way of finding the light pile in each consignment. After some thought a customs officer came up with a neat method which enabled them to find the light pile in each consignment using just one weighing. How was it done?

57 Do you know your birthday?

Perhaps you know on which day of the week you were born. You could hardly be expected to remember the day itself, and your parents may well have forgotten, although you, and they, will know your date of birth. So are you a Wednesday's child, full of woe, or a Monday's child fair of face, or what?

If you had the patience you could carefully count back the days through the years, not forgetting that every fourth year is a leap year, until you arrived at your birthday. That could take a long time. But don't despair, there is a much easier way as follows:

1 Let Y be the year you were born.
2 Let D be the day of the year you were born.
3 Calculate $X = (Y - 1)/4$ and ignore the remainder.
4 Find $S = Y + D + X$
5 Divide S by 7 and note the remainder.

The day on which you were born can now be deduced by using the table below to see which day corresponds to the remainder.

Remainder	0	1	2	3	4	5	6
Birthday	Fri	Sat	Sun	Mon	Tue	Wed	Thur

The following worked example is based on my eldest daughter's birthday and should make the method clear. She was born on the 6th day of June in 1960.

1 $Y = 1960$

2 January 31 days
   February 29 days   as 1960 a leap year
   March   31 days
   April   30 days
   May   31 days
   June   6 days
   $D = 158$

3 $X = \dfrac{1960 - 1}{4} = \dfrac{1959}{4} = 489$ ignoring the remainder

4 $S = 1960 + 158 + 489 = 2607$

5 $2607 \div 7$ gives 372 remainder 3

Using the table, a remainder of 3 would indicate that my daughter was born on a Monday. That was a day I shall never forget as it was a Whitsun Bank Holiday Monday!

When you have found the days on which you and your family and friends were born see if you can see why the method works.

29

58 Ten tors training

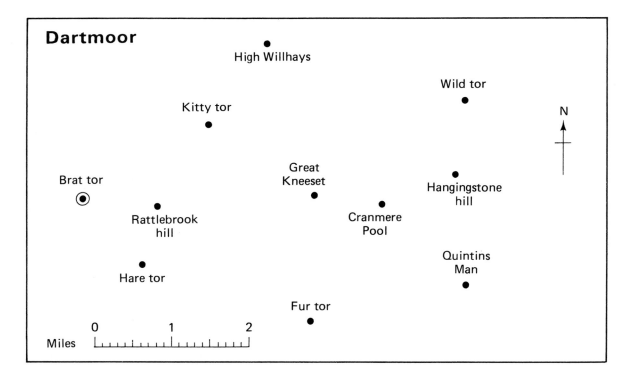

Every year thousands of teenagers take part in the Ten tors expedition which involves walking over Dartmoor and visiting tors (granite outcrops usually found on hilltops) such as those given on the map above. For months in advance of the actual event teams can be found training on the moor every weekend. One weekend a team set out from Brat tor on a map-reading exercise with the object of visiting all the places named on the map shown and returning to their starting point. Find the shortest route they could take.

59 Alphametic puzzles

Solve these where different letters stand for different digits.

```
  C R A M            S A N T A          M A R S
+   C O E          – C L A U S        + B A R S
─────────          ─────────            A R E
  R A C E            X M A S          ─────────
                                        B E S T
```

The solutions are not unique.

60 K9 or One man and his dog

This is a puzzle based on the traditional problem of finding a route for a knight to follow on a chess board which visits each square of the chess board once only. See activity 44 in *The Amazing Mathematical Amusement Arcade* if you are not familiar with knight's tours.

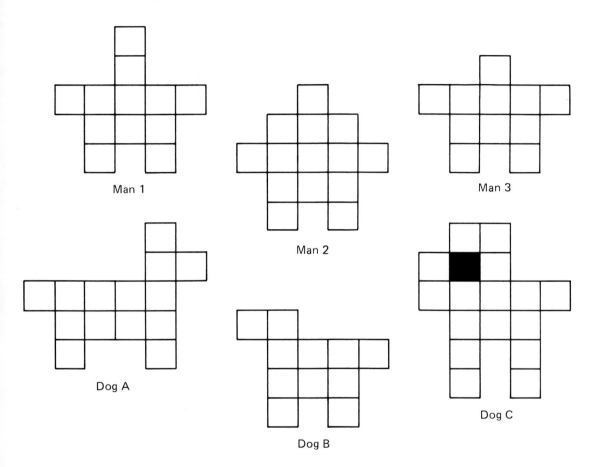

Man 1

Man 2

Man 3

Dog A

Dog B

Dog C

The drawing depicts three men and three dogs, and the object is to pair them off correctly. To do this you must investigate knight's tours on these shapes and decide on which it is

(i) impossible to find a tour
(ii) possible to find a tour
(iii) possible to find a re-entrant tour.

Note that a re-entrant tour is defined as a route which a knight could follow around the shape, visiting each square once, and ending up a knight's move from its starting square.

61 Quadreels

A quadrille is a dance for four couples. Quadreels is a spatial game for a couple to play involving sets of four cotton reels. It is in fact a three-dimensional version of the popular game Connect Four. Before playing the game you will need to construct the playing frame and collect a number of cotton reels.

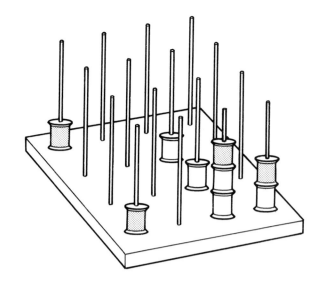

The playing frame consists of a square base board say 15 cm by 15 cm, in which are inserted 16 dowel rods in a 4 × 4 square array (see the diagram). The diameter of the dowel should be about 4 to 5 mm so that a cotton reel can slide down it easily. The length of a dowel above the base board should be sufficient for four cotton reels to stand securely on it.

To play the game you will need up to 64 cotton reels, half of which should be painted red and half blue, or whatever two colours you prefer.

Players take turns to add a reel of their colour to the frame, and the winner is the first person to obtain a line of four of their reels. The line may be horizontal, vertical, or any diagonal so there are many possibilities. A player's turn provides at most 16 possible moves, but deciding which to take to improve your own chance of a line while trying to make sure you stop your opponent needs a lot of skill.

62 Topsy-turvy

Investigate the set of numbers which have the property that when they are multiplied by nine their digits are reversed.

When you have found the underlying pattern to that set of numbers try finding the numbers whose digits are reversed when multiplied by four.

63 Which was the winning strategy?

In a cross-country race four friends each decided on a different strategy towards the way they ran.

Alan decided to run half the distance at 16 km/h and half the distance at 8 km/h.

Bruce ran at 16 km/h for half the time and jogged at 8 km/h for the remaining time.

Christine decided to run at a steady pace of 12 km/h throughout.

Daphne counted her paces as she ran and reckoned to run half of her paces at 16 km/h and the other half at 8 km/h. In what order did they finish?

64 A topological trick

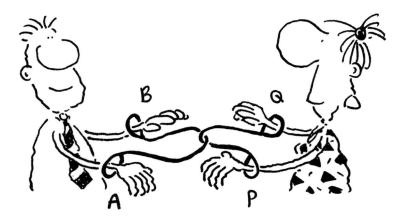

At a party Norman and Nuala were tied together as shown and challenged to separate themselves without untying the string or cutting it. To make it quite clear, Norman has one end of a piece of string tied around his right wrist, *A*, and the other end tied around his left wrist, *B*. Nuala has a second piece of string with one end tied around her left wrist, *P*, and then looped under and over Norman's string before the other end is tied around her right wrist, *Q*. Try it yourself with a friend. It may look impossible to solve at first but there is a neat way of unravelling yourselves which doesn't require any acrobatics.

65 The blanket box

Peter went to a DIY shop to buy some plywood to make a rectangular box in which to store blankets. The shop had a policy of charging at a high rate for cutting into a new sheet of plywood, but at a low rate for offcuts. Peter searched diligently among the stack of offcuts and eventually found three pieces which exactly fulfilled his requirements. One piece was just right for the bottom and a side. Another piece, when cut in two, would make a side and an end. The third piece was just right for the top and the remaining end. The DIY owner worked out the areas of the three pieces (in order to compute their cost) as

   6048 cm²   4563 cm²   and 4995 cm²

Ignoring the thickness of the wood involved, what are the dimensions of the box?

66 Divisibility

Can you arrange the digits 1, 2, 3, 4, 5, 6, 7, 8, 9 in an order so that:

the number formed by the first two digits is divisible by 2
the number formed by the first three digits is divisible by 3
the number formed by the first four digits is divisible by 4
and so on up to nine digits?

The order 1 2 3 6 5 4 9 8 7 looks promising as

   1 2 is divisible by 2
   1 2 3 is divisible by 3
   1 2 3 6 is divisible by 4
   1 2 3 6 5 is divisible by 5
   1 2 3 6 5 4 is divisible by 6

Unfortunately 1 2 3 6 5 4 9 is not divisible by 7. Back to the drawing board and try again!

67 Calculator challenge

The square number 25 has the property that when its digits are increased by 1 it is converted to 36, another square number. There is just one 4-digit square number with the same property. What is it?

68 Toasting efficiently

An old-fashioned electric toaster is only capable of toasting one side each of two pieces of bread at the same time.

Two hands are needed to insert, remove and turn each slice.

The time to toast a side is 30 seconds; the time to turn over a slice is 2 seconds; the time to remove a slice and put it on a plate or to take a slice from the plate and put it in the toaster is 3 seconds. Starting with three slices of bread on a plate, find the minimum time to get three slices of toast on the plate.

69 Playing safe!

A business man called away in a hurry packed his bag in the dark so as not to disturb his wife. He had only two colours of socks in his drawer and, being a methodical person, he knew the drawer contained 10 grey socks and 14 brown socks.

How many socks did he take out to be sure of getting a pair to match?

70 Odds on winning

At a local point-to-point meeting one of the races had only four horses running and the odds offered by the bookmakers are those shown here. Odds of 5 to 2 mean that for every £2 bet the punter wins £5 and has the £2 bet returned, if this horse wins.

How could you lay your bets so that you could be sure that no matter which horse won you would win £10.

	Odds
Brigadoon	2 to 1 favourite
Tophatter	5 to 2
Lightning	6 to 1
Virginsky	6 to 1

71 Tangrams

Start with a square piece of card (8 cm × 8 cm is a convenient size) and cut it into the seven pieces shown.

Now try fitting the pieces together to form the shapes below. Note all seven pieces must be used.

This is an ancient Chinese puzzle which is ageless.

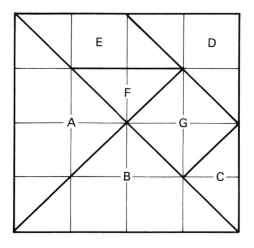

The shapes shown below are just a sample of the hundreds of possible ones. The book by van Delft and Botermans, *Creative Puzzles of the World*, is an excellent reference on this puzzle, known as a tangram, and of many others such as circular and egg-shaped tangrams.

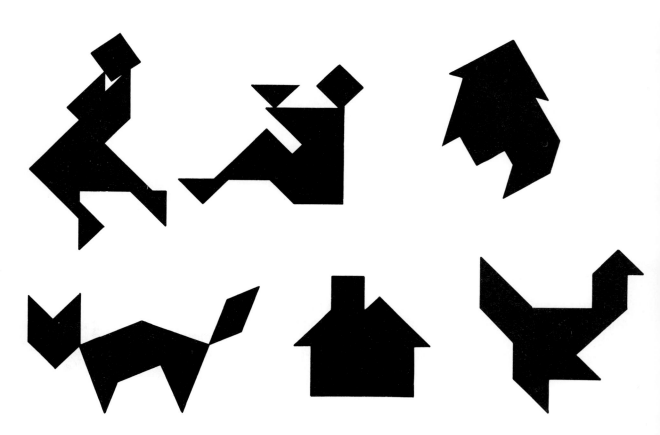

72 Number the sectors

Find numbers A, B, C, D, E, and F for the six sectors so that the number in a sector, or the total of the numbers in a set of adjacent sectors, gives all the integers from 1 to 25 inclusive.

Is it possible to obtain a larger range of numbers in this way?

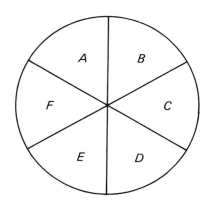

73 Rearranging the hospital ward

A hospital ward contains 16 beds as shown. Using eight screens the ward has been subdivided into four regions containing 8, 3, 3 and 2 beds respectively, categorised by the patients' illnesses. With a new intake it is necessary to subdivide the ward into three regions containing 6, 6 and 4 beds.

What is the smallest number of screens that could be moved to achieve this?

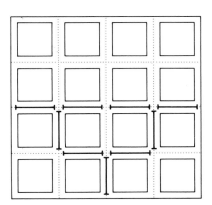

74 One hundred up!

This is a number game for two players involving simple addition. The first player calls a number from 1 to 10. The second player increases this number by any number from 1 to 10.

Players play alternately by always increasing the last number called by any number from 1 to 10. The object is to be the first person to reach 100.

Can you devise a winning strategy?

75 Hidden shapes

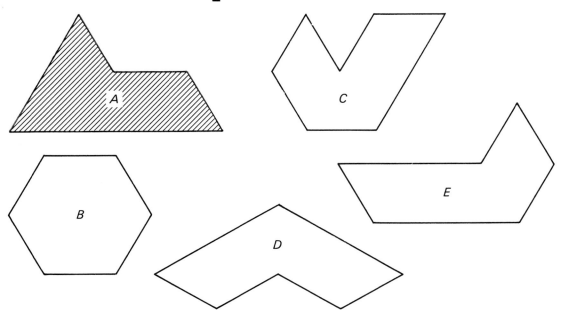

(a) The sphinx-like shape A can be cut into *two* identical
pieces which can be rearranged to form many different
shapes including B, C, D and E. See what different
shapes you can find.

(b) Shape A has the further interesting property that it can
be divided into *four* equal parts which are identical in
shape to A itself. Can you find them?
  What other shapes have this property?

(c) The trapezium shape T can also be obtained from A by
dividing it into two pieces of equal area and rearranging
them. How?

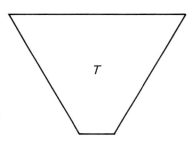

76   Always one short

479 has the interesting property that when it is:

  divided by 6 it leaves a remainder of 5,
  divided by 5 it leaves a remainder of 4,
  divided by 4 it leaves a remainder of 3,
  divided by 3 it leaves a remainder of 2,
  divided by 2 it leaves a remainder of 1.

Which is the smallest number with this property?
  There are three numbers less than 10 000 with the property
that on division by 10, 9, 8, 7, 6, 5, 4, 3 and 2 the remainder
left is always one less than the number divided by. Can you
find them?

77 Amoeboid patterns

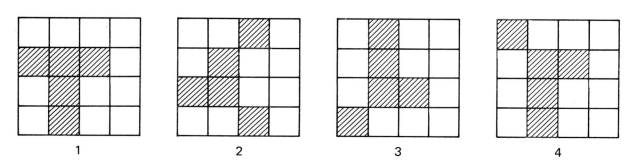

1   2   3   4

Amoebas move by changing their shape. The sequence of shapes above all have the same area and change from one to the next by a simple rule. Find the rule and give the next two shapes. Will the shape ever return to its original position?

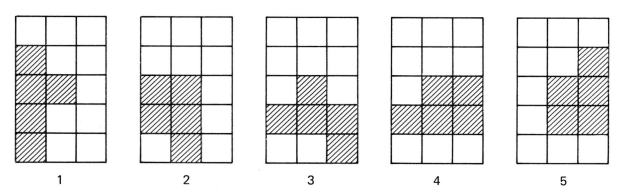

1   2   3   4   5

Spot the rule in this second amoeboid pattern and investigate the different shapes which are generated.

Try making up rules of your own to generate shapes.

78 The Embassy reception

There were 80 ambassadors at the Utopian Embassy's reception. By the end of the evening every one of the ambassadors had been formally introduced and shaken hands with every other ambassador. How many handshakes took place?

39

79 Quartering a circle

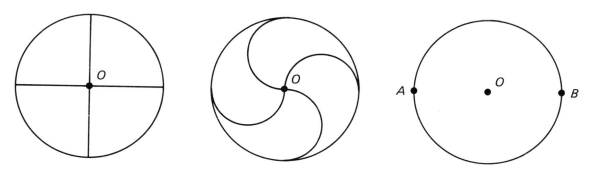

A circle can be divided into four parts of equal area in many ways, two of which are shown above. See what other ways you can find of doing this.

Now see if you can find a way of drawing three curves from A to B, of equal length, which do not cross each other and divide the circle above into four equal areas.

80 Sweeping the park efficiently

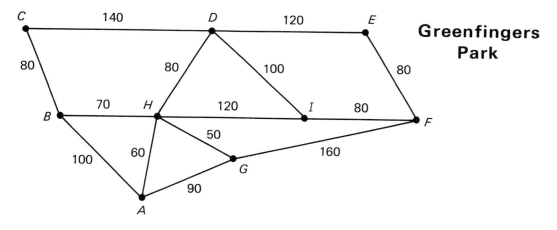

Greenfingers Park

The map above shows the paths in an inner city park, with their lengths given in metres. Each day before the park is open to the public a council worker drives around all the paths with a mechanical road sweeper. The sweeper is housed at H and the worker is annoyed because no matter what route is followed it does not seem possible to sweep all the paths without retracing some. Is this inevitable?

What is the shortest distance which the sweeper can take to sweep all the paths and return to H?

81 Pentomino parcels

For Xmas a large London store decided to pack its gifts into boxes whose horizontal cross-sections were in the shape of the pentominoes. They were then able to assemble a large variety of Xmas hampers with a square (5×5) cross-section each containing five presents. One such hamper is shown. Also shown are the 12 pentomino boxes and their contents.

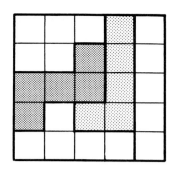

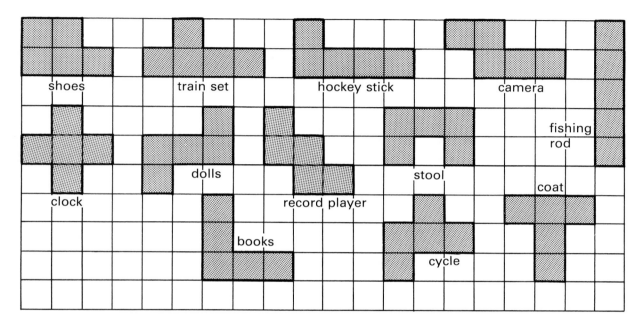

shoes train set hockey stick camera fishing rod dolls stool coat clock record player cycle books

The parents of a pair of twins Lucy and Philip put in an order for two hampers with the proviso that Lucy's should contain a clock and that neither twin should have a present in common. What did they each get?
It is taken for granted that the five boxes in each hamper are different.

82 A stamp book with a difference

One GPO stamp designer, more out of curiosity than practicality, decided to design a book with six stamps in a 3×2 page in such a way that by removing a single stamp or a connected set of stamps it would be possible to match all possible postage rates 1p, 2p, 3p, . . ., Np where N was to be as large as possible. There would be no conditions on the values of stamps which were allowed and his first solution is shown here. The designer was very pleased with it to start with for it seemed possible to tear off a stamp or a connected set of stamps for all values from 1p to 32p. However, on checking there was one value which could not be made up. (Note that the stamps must be connected by their edges.)

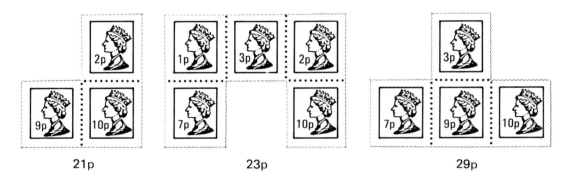

| 21p | 23p | 29p |

The diagram shows connected sets of stamps which give totals of 21p, 23p and 29p respectively. Check all the other totals from 1p to 32p and find which one is not possible.

Eventually the designer found values for the stamps which made it possible to get further than 32p and without any gaps. How far can you get?

83 Some curious number relations

$$43 = 4^2 + 3^3$$
$$135 = 1^1 + 3^2 + 5^3$$
$$518 = 5^1 + 1^2 + 8^3$$
$$2427 = 2^1 + 4^2 + 2^3 + 7^4$$

See if you can find any more with similar patterns.

84 Concentric magic squares

The 5×5 magic square given here has the fascinating property that the 3×3 array of numbers at its centre is also a magic square.

This is not the only way in which the numbers 1 to 25 can be arranged to form a 5×5 magic square which includes a 3×3 magic square at its centre. Another one can be found by forming a 3×3 magic square from the numbers

    5,6,7,12,13,14,19,20,21

and then suitably placing the missing numbers around its border. See what you can find.

The concept of magic squares within squares can be extended. When the adjoining 9×9 magic square is completed it will contain each of the numbers 1 to 81 and also contain within itself:

a 7×7 magic square
a 5×5 magic square
and a 3×3 magic square

23	1	2	20	19
22	16	9	14	4
5	11	13	15	21
8	12	17	10	18
7	25	24	6	3

2			13	77			81	16
	18				62	65		
7			35		53		23	
		32	38		40	50		74
73	57			41			25	
	22				44	34		10
68		46				52	63	
67	54		56	21				
		70			4	3		80

85 Connecting the fire hydrants

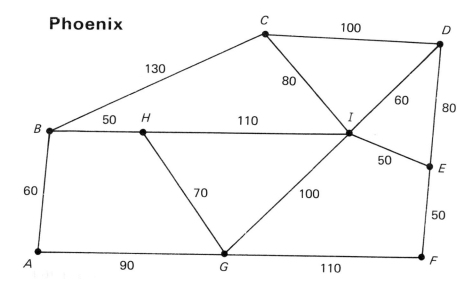

Phoenix

The town of Phoenix was notorious for the number of its houses that were lost due to fires. To overcome this bad reputation the town councillors drew up a plan to site nine fire hydrants at the points shown on the above map. To ensure sufficient water pressure at these hydrants it was decided to lay a new water main to interconnect them all. Digging trenches to put in the necessary pipes was going to be very expensive so the town councillors decided to hold a competition to see who could devise the shortest water main to connect all the hydrants. Because of the existing buildings the pipes could only be placed along the lines shown on the map. The length of each line in metres is given on the map.

Would you have won the competition?

86 To set you thinking

Twelve matches are arranged like a hexagonal wheel to form six identical equilateral triangles. Show how to move just four matches to form three equilateral triangles.

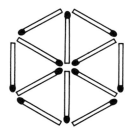

44

87 Kirkman's schoolgirls problem

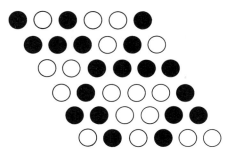

This problem was first proposed by T.P. Kirkman in the *Lady's and Gentleman's Diary* for 1850 and it has since been subject to much analysis by numerous puzzlers and mathematicians.

The puzzle concerns the house-mistress of a girls' boarding school who took her 15 girls for a walk daily. They always walked in crocodile in 5 rows with 3 abreast. From her experience over many years the house-mistress had devised a scheme whereby each girl had two different walking companions on each day of the week.

Before trying this question try solving the similar one applying to 9 boys walking in 3 rows with 3 abreast who are to have different walking companions on 4 days.

88 Spot the pattern

At a first glance there may seem to be no rhyme or reason in the pattern of black and white circles. But the pattern is generated from the top row, by a simple rule where each new row is worked out from the row immediately above it.

When you have spotted the pattern complete several more rows and see if you can decide whether a row could ever consist of:

    all white circles
    all black circles
    one black circle.

Does the pattern in a row ever repeat itself?
    Investigate what happens starting off with

      (*a*) a different pattern of circles in the first row,
      (*b*) a different number of circles in the first row.

89   Two of a kind

Some games which, on the face of it have nothing in common turn out to be structurally identical. The following games for two players form such a group.

1 Take a pack of playing cards and from it extract the ace and 2 to 9 of diamonds. Lay these nine cards face upwards on the table and, with ace counting as 1, players in turn pick a card from the table. The first person to hold *three* cards which total 15 is the winner.

2 Print each of the nine words on a card as shown and place them face up on the table.

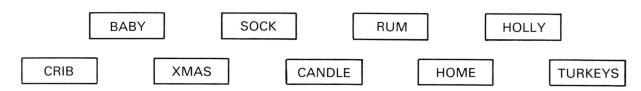

BABY	SOCK	RUM	HOLLY

CRIB	XMAS	CANDLE	HOME	TURKEYS

Players, in turn, pick a card off the table. The first person to hold *three* cards containing the same letter wins.

90   Carving up the camels

On his deathbed the elderly arab gathered his three sons around him and expressed his wish that his 23 prize camels should be shared among them. Ahab the eldest was to have half of the camels, Aziz the second son was to have a third and Abdul the youngest was to have an eighth share. Initially pleased with their lot the sons soon realised they had a problem for they couldn't see how they could divide 23 camels into their allotted shares without slaughtering some of them. In their anguish they turned to their late father's revered brother for advice. After sleeping on the problem he lent them one of his own prize camels thus making a total of 24 and suggested they shared them out. Ahab took 12, his half share, Azis then took 8, his third, and Abdul then took 3, his eighth share, and then returned his uncle's camel to him with much thanks. Where is the catch?

91 Thwaites' conjecture

When Bryan Thwaites was a schoolmaster in the early 1950s he set his pupils a task of investigating the sequence of numbers produced when if a number was even it was halved and if it was odd it was multiplied by 3 and then increased by 1.

For example, if 7 is taken as the starting point then

$$7 \text{ odd} \rightarrow 7 \times 3 + 1 = 22$$
$$22 \text{ even} \rightarrow 22 \div 2 \quad = 11$$
$$11 \text{ odd} \rightarrow 11 \times 3 + 1 = 34$$
$$34 \text{ even} \rightarrow 34 \div 2 \quad = 17$$
$$17 \text{ odd} \rightarrow 17 \times 3 + 1 = 52$$
$$52 \text{ even} \rightarrow 52 \div 2 \quad = 26$$
$$26 \text{ even} \rightarrow 26 \div 2 \quad = 13$$

and so on.

Clearly an odd number leads to a larger number, but it will necessarily be even, so at the next stage it will be halved.

From the pupils' investigations at the time, and his own researches since, Bryan Thwaites believes that the sequence will eventually reach 1, at which point it would keep cycling through the sequence 421421421… so 1 can be taken as the end point. Many mathematicians around the world have tried to prove this conjecture, or alternatively find a different end point, but so far without success.

Continue the above sequence until it reaches 1 and then investigate the process with other starting points.

92 A fascinating family of square numbers

$$1\ 6 \qquad\qquad = 4^2$$
$$1\ 1\ 5\ 6 \qquad\quad = 34^2$$
$$1\ 1\ 1\ 5\ 5\ 6 \qquad = 334^2$$
$$1\ 1\ 1\ 1\ 5\ 5\ 5\ 6 \quad = 3334^2$$
$$1\ 1\ 1\ 1\ 1\ 5\ 5\ 5\ 5\ 6 = 33334^2$$

Each number in this sequence is obtained from the previous one by inserting 15 in the middle like the extra leaf in an expanding table. Can you show why the numbers in this sequence will always be square no matter how far you go.

There is one other sequence of numbers like this one. See if you can find it.

93 Playing detective

When a teacher's telephone bill arrived she noticed with interest that the number of pounds was a factor of her telephone number. What's more, she realized that the remaining factors corresponded to the size of her fifth year mathematics class and to the number of her children.

Her telephone number was 18998 and you might be interested to know she had one more son than she had daughters.

What can you find out about her?

94 Community coppers

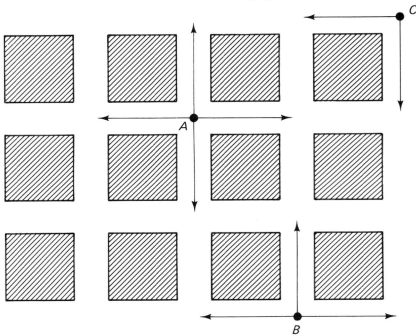

A city police force has to keep its blocks of buildings under constant surveillance at night on all sides. The blocks are all the same size, square, and in a regular pattern as shown. Each police constable can see only the length of one block. For example, a constable at A can see two sides of each of the four blocks which meet at that cross roads. A constable at B on the edge of the city can only watch two sides on each of two blocks however, while a constable at C could only watch two sides of one block.

The problem is to find the smallest number of police constables who could keep a watch on the above 4 × 3 city.

95 The shunting yard

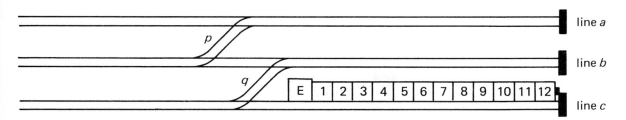

line a

line b

| E | 1 | 2 | 3 | 4 | 5 | 6 | 7 | 8 | 9 | 10 | 11 | 12 |

line c

Three parallel tracks in a shunting yard, a, b and c, are connected by short tracks p and q. There are twelve trucks numbered 1 to 12 on line c, see the diagram, and it is required that trucks numbered 3, 7, 10 and 11 are shunted onto line a by the engine on line c to make up a train for a new destination. How would you do this in the most efficient way possible, that is with the fewest shunts? The remaining trucks and engine are to end up on line c.

96 A symmetric cross-number puzzle

An 8×8 cross-number puzzle has most of its black squares missing but they can soon be filled in with the knowledge that the completed puzzle is symmetric about the two dotted lines shown. To complete the puzzle all you need to know is that every number is either prime or the cube of a prime, and that only three different digits appear in the solution.

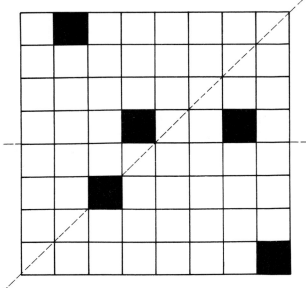

97 Intersecting lines

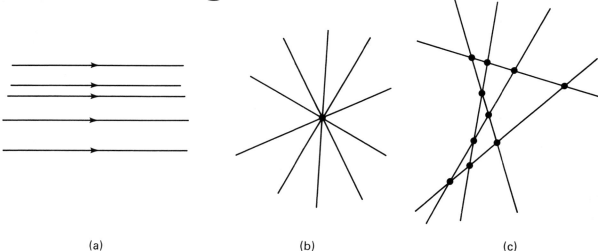

(a) (b) (c)

Five straight lines can be drawn in a plane in an infinite
number of ways. They could be parallel as in (a) when they
do not cross anywhere, or all pass through one point as in (b).
The largest number of intersections obtainable is 10 as in (c).

How many different ways can you find to draw 5 lines with
only 8 intersections?

Now show how to draw 10 lines so that they make 27
intersections.

98 One-upmanship!

Christopher and Elizabeth were working together on a
project about square numbers when Christopher announced
that he had found something very special about the squares of
the eight numbers

$$7, 8, 9, 10, 11, 12, 13, 14.$$

He found that they could be divided into two sets of four
whose totals exactly matched:

$$7^2 + 10^2 + 12^2 + 13^2 = 462 = 8^2 + 9^2 + 11^2 + 14^2$$

He sat back, proud of his find, but Elizabeth took a closer
look at the numbers. She first wondered whether the fact that
14 was double 7 was important but after further
investigation, decided that this was a red herring and tried
looking at the squares of 5, 6, 7, 8, 9, 10, 11, 12. She found
that these could also be put into two sets with equal totals and
began to speculate that it might always be possible with the
squares of eight consecutive whole numbers. Is she right?

50

99 The Grand Prix circuit

The plan of a Grand Prix car racing circuit is as shown. Every time a car rounds a bend the wheels on the outside of the bend travel further than those on the inside. If the distance between the inner and outer wheels of a car is 2 metres, how much further do the outer wheels travel on one lap of this circuit?

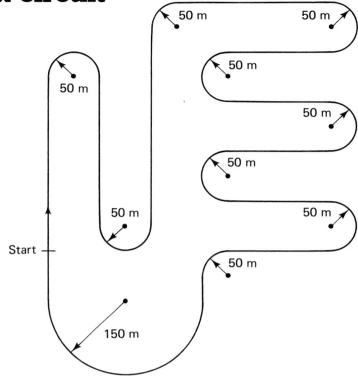

100 Robotics

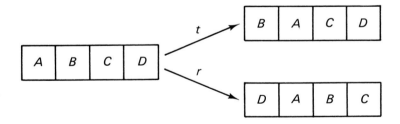

At a point on a production line four components arrive in order *ABCD* but may be required at the next stage in any order. To achieve the order required a robot has been programmed to do two basic operations:

   t: interchange the first two components
   r: move the last component to the front and push them
      all back one space.

These operations are represented by the diagram above.

   How can the robot's two basic operations be used to produce the order *DACB*?

101   Think again!

```
1
1  1
2  1
1  2  1  1
1  1  1  2  2  1
3  1  2  2  1  1
1  3  1  1  2  2  2  1
```

What is the next line?

In which line does 4 occur first.

The step from one line to the next is very logical and not difficult, but can you spot it?

102   Squared sums!

D. St P. Barnard regularly sets puzzles in *The Daily Telegraph* and set one recently based on the intriguing relation

$$(6048 + 1729)^2 = 60\,481\,729$$

There is another pair of 4-digit numbers with the same property but without a microcomputer you may take a long time to find it. However similar properties exist for pairs of single-digit number and pairs of 2-digit numbers which are much more accessible. Investigate all the solutions to

$$(a + b)^2 = ab \quad \text{where } ab \quad \text{is a 2-digit number,}$$
$$(ab + cd)^2 = abcd \text{ where } abcd \text{ is a 4-digit number.}$$

103   A doubly magic triangle

The numbers 1,2,3, . . ., 9 can be put into the circles on the triangle in many ways so that their sum along each side is the same. But can you find such an arrangement where the sums of the squares along each side are also equal to one another?

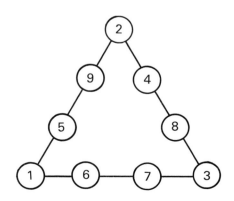

104 The travelling salesman problem

There are many times when people have to visit a number of different places and then return to the starting point. They will often want to find the shortest possible route. Such a situation is called *the travelling salesman problem*, for it is one which salesmen face on most days of their working lives.

It is, however, a problem which many people would like to solve: for example,
— the oil-tanker driver who has to take petrol to a number of different filling stations,
— the driver of a milk-tanker who has to visit scattered farms,
— the American tourist who wants to visit Cambridge, Stratford-on-Avon, Edinburgh, Plymouth and Stonehenge.

Consider Mrs Lavender, a saleswoman based in Exeter, who has to visit the local towns shown on the map (a) to sell cosmetics. The numbers on the roads give the distance in miles between the towns. What is the shortest route she can take which will both start and end at Exeter?

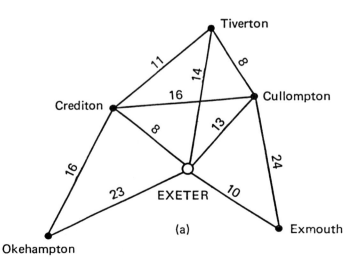

(a)

One popular method used to solve this type of problem is the *nearest city* approach. This means that Mrs Lavender will begin by going to the nearest town to Exeter. This is Crediton. Next she goes to the nearest town to Crediton she has not already visited and so on. This leads to the solution shown in (b). First we have the loop Exeter, Crediton, Tiverton, Cullompton, Exmouth and back to Exeter. After that there is the short loop Exeter, Okehampton, Exeter.

The total distance following this route is 107 miles, which is not the shortest. In practice it may use better roads and be the quickest, but we are only looking for the shortest distance. Can you find the shortest route?

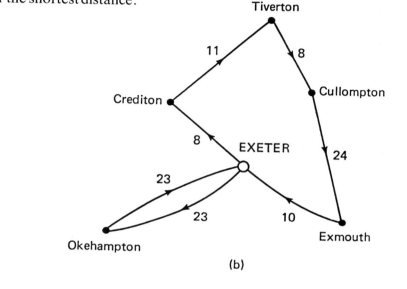

(b)

Suppose Mrs Lavender adds Honiton to the list of towns she will visit. What will now be the shortest route visiting all the towns (starting and ending at Exeter)? Could Mrs Lavender find a shorter route if she started and finished at Cullompton?

Does it make any difference which town you start and finish at?

If Mrs Lavender did not have to finish at the town where she started, which towns should she start and end at to give the shortest route?

Mathematicians have tried hard to find ways of solving problems like these. So far they have been unsuccessful. They know that a shortest route cannot cross itself. However, the methods they know for finding exact solutions are no use for complicated problems with many towns.

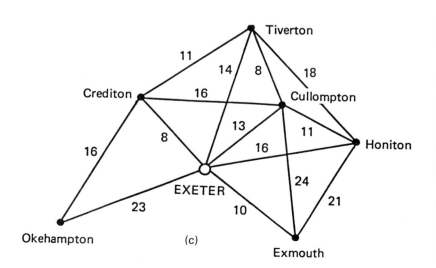

(c)

54

105 Ever more triangles and squares

Take six drinking straws and cut them in half to give twelve short straws. Arrange them to make the two equilateral triangles shown.

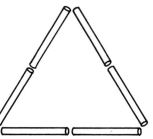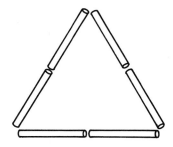

How else could you make two equilateral triangles using all of the short straws?

Using all twelve of your short straws in each case show how to make:

(*a*) one equilateral triangle
(*b*) three equilateral triangles
(*c*) four equilateral triangles
(*d*) five equilateral triangles
(*e*) six equilateral triangles
(*f*) eight equilateral triangles

(*g*) one square
(*h*) two squares
(*i*) three squares
(*j*) five squares
(*k*) six squares
(*l*) three squares and eight triangles

106 Edging along the octahedron

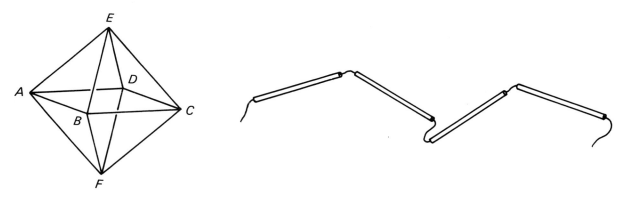

Starting from one vertex of an octahedron, say *A*, it is possible to find a route along all its edges and return to the starting point without having to retrace any edge, for example

$$A \rightarrow B \rightarrow E \rightarrow D \rightarrow F \rightarrow B \rightarrow C \rightarrow D \rightarrow A \rightarrow E \rightarrow C \rightarrow F \rightarrow A$$

How many such paths are there which start at A?

The fact that such paths exist means that it is possible to make an edge model of an octahedron by first making a closed loop of twelve straws threaded on a length of shirring elastic, and then tying the loop together at six points corresponding to the vertices. Make one for yourself!

107 Toilet tissue thickness

An accountant was always on the lookout for a bargain when she did her shopping. One day she saw that Sainsbury's had a special line selling packs with 4 rolls of toilet tissues, with 240 sheets in each roll. Knowing how particular her sons were about the thickness of the tissues they liked to use, she tried to work out the thickness of these particular tissues so that she could compare them with those she usually purchased.

She knew the tissues were 14 cm long and she estimated the diameter of the rolls as 11 cm, each wound on cardboard cylinders of diameter 4 cm. At first she was concerned at the fact that the tissues were wound onto the roll in a spiral with increasing radius, but it wasn't long before she saw her way around this problem and calculated the tissue's thickness. How thick was the tissue?

About how many turns of paper are there on each roll?

108 Fun with subtraction

The square pattern shown was obtained by putting the numbers 1, 25, 37 and 28 at the corners of a square. By joining the midpoints of its sides, a smaller square was drawn inside the first square. Each corner of this new square was allocated a number by finding the difference between the two numbers at the ends of the line on which it stands (eg, 37–25 = 12, 37–28 = 9). This new square was then taken as the starting point and the process was repeated until the numbers in the corners were the same – in this case 6. What is the longest sequence of squares that you can find?

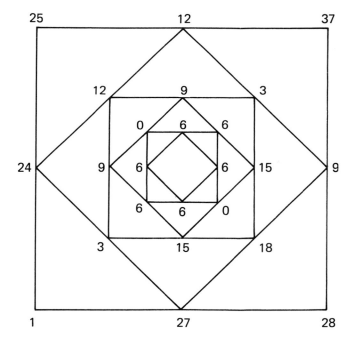

109   Make a century

$$96 + \frac{2148}{537} = 100$$

There are eleven ways in which the digits 1, 2, ..., 9 can be
arranged as a whole number plus a rational number whose
sum is 100. One of these ways is shown above. See how many
of the others you can find.

110   Know your cube

Find the angle between the two dotted lines drawn on the
surfaces of a cube.

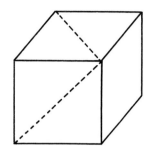

111   Mixed doubles

The village tennis club was quite a modest affair having only
two courts. On one Saturday afternoon only eight players
turned up to play,

Adrian, Bernard, Colin, David

Amanda, Brenda, Carole and Doris.

Carole, the club secretary, always ready to organise, soon
proposed a plan for mixed doubles. Her plan envisaged
everyone playing three matches in such a way that no one
ever had the same partner twice or the same opponent twice.
The ingenuity of this plan pleased everyone so it was readily
accepted.

What was Carole's plan?

112 Siting the airport terminal

AB, BC and CA represent three runways at a busy airport. It is planned to site a new terminal building at a point P so that the total distance of the approach runways to be built

$$PN + PL + PM$$

is a minimum.

ABC is an equilateral triangle, and the new runways are perpendicular to the main runways. Where should P be sited?

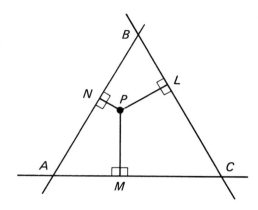

113 Reconstructing the manor house

Some historians were trying to piece together evidence, from a variety of sources, on an old manor house, long since destroyed. They knew that one of the main rooms had a long wall completely oak panelled, while its end wall opposite the doorway was covered by a tapestry purchased in France. The floor had been covered by a specially made Persian carpet. Many details of the design and colours were known in each case, and they knew the areas of the panelling, the tapestry and the carpet were 72m², 32m² and 144m². Nowhere, however, could they find any reference to the linear dimensions of the room. Can you help them?

114 Who came in second?

Tom, Dick and Harry engage in some track and field events in which points are awarded for 1st, 2nd and 3rd. At the end of the events Tom has 22 points, while Dick and Harry both have 9 points. No-one else had any points. Dick was 1st in the javelin throw. Who came 2nd in the 100 metres?

115 Chess board tours

Although the activities here are described in terms of a chess board and chess pieces all that is required is some squared paper, a pencil, and the basic knowledge of how a chess piece moves.

Rook's tours

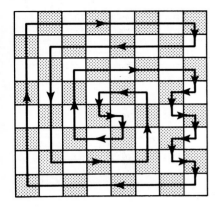 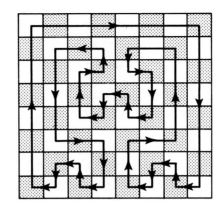

A rook can move to right or left, or up or down only. Investigate routes which a rook can follow on a chess board which enable it to visit every square once and return to its starting point. Such routes, which form continuous loops are called re-entrant. Two solutions are given to start you off.

What is the smallest number of changes of direction required by a rook to complete a re-entrant tour?

If a rook's tour is not required to be re-entrant then it can visit each square once with only fourteen changes of direction. Can you find such a route?

Is it possible for a rook to start at one corner, enter every square once, and finish in the opposite corner?

Queen's tours

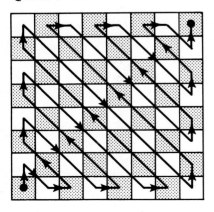 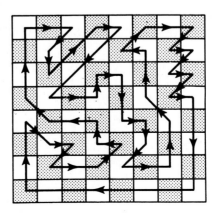

A queen can move diagonally as well as to and fro and up and down like a rook, so its tours can have more variety. The first example of a queen's tour shown here is symmetric and travels from one corner to another, while the second one has no pretence to symmetry but is re-entrant.

Investigate symmetric re-entrant tours.

If the queen is allowed to visit a square more than once then it is possible for her to make a re-entrant tour of the board with only thirteen changes of direction. See if you can find such a solution.

The queen's tour shown right has the fascinating property that if the squares are numbered consecutively, as they are visited, starting with 1 in the square marked S, then it will be a magic square. Test it for yourself.

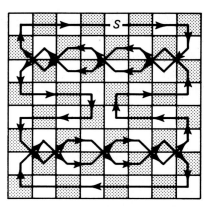

The queen's magic tour

Bishop's tours

Bishops are restricted to diagonal movements only, so if a bishop starts on a black square it can only move to another black square. Even then, it is not possible to visit all the black squares on the board without re-visiting some of them on the way. Why?

The tour shown here misses out on six black squares. You can do better than this!

If you allow the bishop to revisit some squares then it is possible to start at one corner, visit every black square and end in the opposite corner on a route consisting of seventeen lines. How?

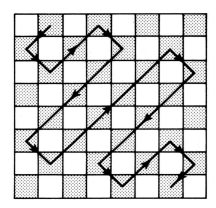

116 Amaze your friends

Ask one of your friends for two 6 figure numbers, a and b. Write these down and under them write a number a* of your own choosing. Now ask for a different 6 figure number c, which you write down and then add another number c* also of your choosing, before quickly writing down the total of all the five numbers.

How are a and c connected to a* and c*, and how is the total connected to b?

```
  7 2 8 4 6 1   a
  3 7 6 5 9 8   b
+ 2 7 1 5 3 8   a*
  8 5 4 7 5 0   c
  1 4 5 2 4 9   c*
  ───────────
2 3 7 6 5 9 6
```

117 Court card capers

Take all the Jacks, Queens, Kings and Aces from a pack of playing cards and arrange them in a 4×4 square array so that each row and each column contains exactly one card of each rank. One solution is shown but there are many more.

Now find a solution in which the diagonals as well as the rows and columns contain only one card of each rank.

But the real puzzle is to find a solution where there is only one card of each suit as well as only one card of each rank in every row, column and diagonal. There are 72 solutions ... take your pick!

Ace	King	Queen	Jack
King	Queen	Jack	Ace
Jack	Ace	King	Queen
Queen	Jack	Ace	King

118 Crossing the desert

A group of students organise an expedition to explore the interior of a vast desert region. They arrive at the edge of the desert with supplies (petrol, water, food etc.) for a journey of 1600 miles. Unfortunately they only have one lorry, and fully laden it can only carry sufficient supplies for 400 miles.

What is the greatest distance they can travel into the desert and return safely?

119 Don't be square

Four counters can be put on a 5 × 5 board so that they lie at the vertices of a square in many ways. Two are shown here, but how many are there altogether?

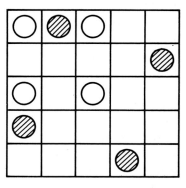

What is the largest number of counters which you can put on the board so that no four counters lie at the vertices of a square?

You could make an interesting game out of this for two or three players. Each player adds a counter to the board in turn and is eliminated if this counter forms a square with three other counters already on the board. The winner is the last person to play a counter which does not form a square.

120 Can you help the motorway designer?

Four large towns lie at the vertices of a square of side 20 miles. Because of the growing importance of trade between the towns the government decided to design a motorway network to connect all the towns to each other. Naturally, the government wanted to keep the cost to a minimum, so they insisted that the engineers made the motorway as short as possible.

The engineers considered the merit of a variety of solutions, such as the three shown here, and

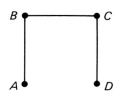
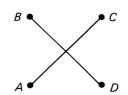

soon came to the conclusion that the best solution would be to have a motorway along the two diagonals AC and BD which required 56.6 miles of carriageway which they thought was the shortest solution. But they were wrong. There is a better solution. Can you find it?

121 Look before you leap!

1 Which weighs heavier, 50 kilograms of feathers or 50 kilograms of coal?

2 How much earth is there in a hole in the ground which is 25m long, 6m wide and 2m deep?

3 A ship stood at anchor outside a port. To make access for visitors easier a rope ladder was hung over the side. The rungs of the ladder were 0.4m apart, and at 10 a.m., 12 rungs of the ladder were above the water. The tide was rising at a rate of 1.2m an hour, so the lady mayoress of the port delayed her visit to the ship until 1.00 p.m. by when, she argued, she would have fewer rungs to climb. How many rungs did she climb assuming that the tide continued to rise at the same rate, and that she arrived on time?

4 A squash racket and a ball together cost £31.60. The racket cost £30 more than the ball. What did the ball cost?

5 A farmer, who had been plagued by rabbits, went out early one evening armed with his shot gun. He found 13 rabbits feeding in his corn field and with his first shot killed one. How many rabbits remained in the field?

122 What's wrong?

Let $x = y$ be any non-zero number. Then multiplying through by x gives

$$x^2 = xy$$

and subtracting y^2 gives

$$x^2 - y^2 = xy - y^2$$

factorising both sides leads to

$$(x - y)(x + y) = (x - y)y$$

and then dividing through by the common factor leaves

$$x + y = y$$

But $y = x$ so

$$2x = x$$

and as x is non-zero we must conclude that

$$2 = 1$$

Where is the flaw in the argument?

123 Calendar capers

Because the numbers on a calendar occur in 7 columns there is a regularity about their pattern which can be exploited in some simple tricks.

Ask someone to add together three numbers which come immediately beneath each other in a column and give the total. Suppose the total came to 45 then you can very quickly give them the three dates they have added, for the middle date is ⅓ of the total (i.e. 15) and the other dates are 7 each side of it (i.e. 8 and 22).

What were the dates when the total given was 57?

How could you adapt the method if someone gave you the total for five numbers in a column?

One of the columns of five numbers above totals 85. Which one? You should have no need to add up any of the columns.

When you start looking at the pages of calendars, no matter for which month or year, you will realise that the same numbers always occur underneath one another for they step up in 7s, so, for example, 18 is always below 11 and 25 always below 18.

Why can't a column which starts with 6 have five numbers in it?

Can you devise a method to give the dates when you are told the total of four numbers which came underneath each other?

Relationships can easily be established between the dates inside a 2 × 2 square or 3 × 3 square and their totals.

With a 2 × 2 square for example the total is always

$$4 \times (\text{smallest date} + 4)$$

and this can be used both ways:

(a) ask someone to give you the total and then you give the dates

or

(b) ask someone to give you the smallest number and then you give them the total.

Why does it work?

Suppose the smallest date is D then the four dates are

D	$D+1$
$D+7$	$D+8$

with a total of $T = 4D + 16$ which is equal to $4(D+4)$.

Suppose you were given the total T then to find D first divide by 4 to find $D+4$ then subtract 4.

Sun	Mon	Tue	Wed	Thu	Fri	Sat
				1	2	3
4	5	6	7	8	9	10
11	12	13	14	15	16	17
18	19	20	21	22	23	24
25	26	27	28	29	30	31

Sun	Mon	Tue	Wed	Thu	Fri	Sat
	1	2	3	4	5	6
7	8	9	10	11	12	13
14	15	16	17	18	19	20
21	22	23	24	25	26	27
28	29	30	31			

124 Optimising

The number 17 can be expressed as the sum of positive numbers in many ways, for example

$$17 = 6 + 11 = 2 + 3 + 5 + 7$$

Now consider the product of the numbers used in the decomposition in each case:

$$6 \times 11 = 66 \qquad 2 \times 3 \times 5 \times 7 = 210$$

The challenge is to find the decomposition of 17 into a set of positive numbers which yields the largest product.

125 How not to cancel

In a lesson on simplifying fractions Jane saw the two 6s in the fraction $\frac{26}{65}$ and crossed them out.

$$\frac{2\cancel{6}}{\cancel{6}5} = \frac{2}{5}$$

When the teacher read out the answers at the end of the lesson Jane proudly ticked her answer. How many other fractions of the form $\frac{ab}{bc}$ can you find where crossing out the bs will leave the correct answer $\frac{a}{c}$? You may ignore the trivial solutions where $a = b = c$.

126 Integers only

Investigating triangles whose sides and whose areas were integers a student found to her surprise that she had discovered three such triangles whose area was 84 square units. Can you find them?

127 Box designing

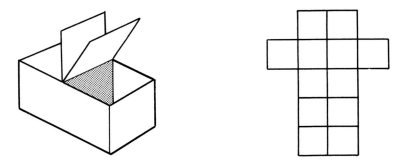

A cardboard box manufacturer asked his designers to produce a suitable net for a box equivalent to two cubes with a partition down the middle and two lids as shown. There are many possible designs which you can find for yourself, but the design eventually used by the manufacturer was based on the cross shown.

Show how, by making two cuts in the cross, it can be folded to form the required box complete with its lids.

128 A multitude of magic squares

Starting with 5, 8 and 12 in the positions shown the magic square can be completed uniquely as shown by knowing that the magic total is always 3 times the number in the centre. The challenge is to find all the different 3×3 magic squares which contain, 5, 8, and 12.

COMMENTARY

1 Matchstick magic

In solving matchstick puzzles most people start with a hit or miss approach, but a little bit of analysis can pay dividends. Here there are 24 matches so removing 4 leaves 20. If exactly five identical squares have to be formed then it indicates the need to look for five squares which have no matchstick in common. As matches are only being removed, the arrangement must already exist within the original array and the solution is shown here. The smallest number of matches that can be removed to leave just two squares is eight: the outside 3×3 square and the middle square.

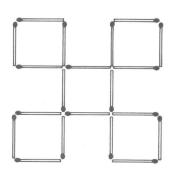

2 The car jam

Take the width of a car as 1 unit, its length as 2 units, and L, R, U, D to mean left, right, up, down respectively.

Then car 1 will be released by the following car moves: 3(L1), 4(U1), 5(R2), 11(U2), 6(U1), 7(U2), 12(L4), 8(L1), 13(U1), 10(R1), 1(D6). The key to the solution is to appreciate that 10 must move to the right which can only be achieved by moving 13 up, which in turn requires that 12 moves left etc.

Try making similar puzzles of your own.

3 Who nobbled the racehorse?

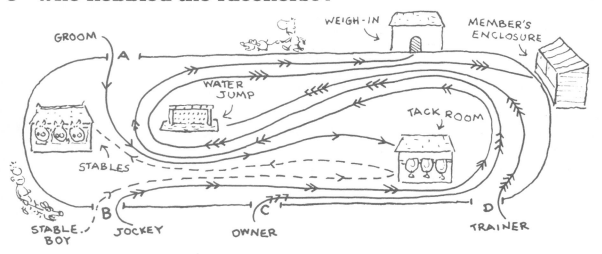

Putting all the evidence available on the diagram of the racecourse leads to the groom as being the guilty party. The jockey's route excludes the owner and the trainer, while the fact that the stable lad and the groom met at the tack room excludes the jockey.

4 The car importer

This puzzle depends on the fact that 1 111 111 is the
product of just two prime factors: 4649 and 239. Thus
there were 239 new cars each costing £4649. Theoretically
4649 cars at £239 is a possible but unrealistic answer.

5 Number pyramids

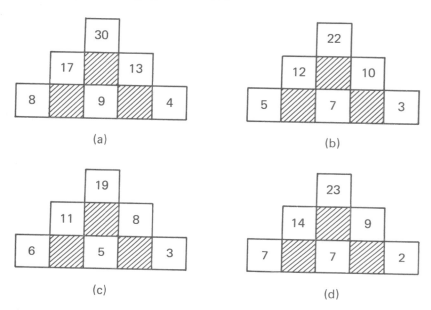

(a)

(b)

(c)

(d)

6 The triangular building site

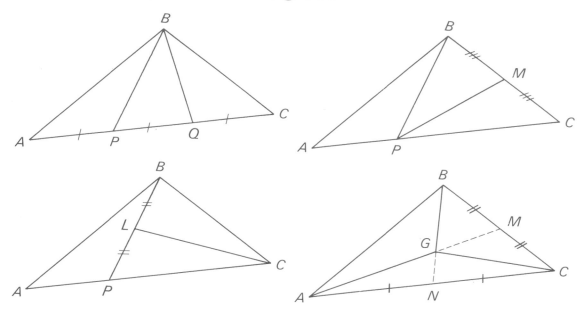

7 Ring the triangle

    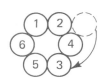

8 The jeweller's chain

There are seven pieces to join so the obvious solution would appear to be to cut a link on six of the pieces and use it to add another piece of the chain thus taking 2 hours.

A better solution is to cut all the links of the piece which had 5 links and use those links to join together the remaining six pieces thus taking 1 hour and 40 minutes.

The best solution however is to cut the 4 links of the two pieces which had 2 links and use these to join together the remaining five pieces thus needing only 1 hour and 20 minutes.

The jeweller could thus have gone home at 6.20 pm.

9 The anti-litter campaign

11 bins are required to ensure 3 on each path. The solution is indicated by the small circles which occur at all the 10 points where four paths intersect, and where two paths intersect at the middle of the bottom end of the park.

Only four park attendants would be required to ensure the presence of at least one on each path and their placing is indicated by the letter P on the diagram.

This puzzle is best tackled by making a drawing of the plan of the paths and experimenting with positioning counters at intersections to aid one's thinking.

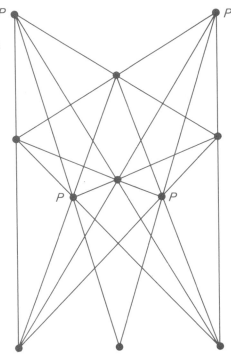

10 The railcar terminus

The solution to this puzzle depends on appreciating that the effect of driving a set of railcars around the loop is that they re-enter the main line in the opposite order to that which they left it. To put railcar 7 in the position to depart first requires, initially, that it is positioned on the left hand end of the line of railcars, by driving 1, 2, . . . 7 around the loop, and then to drive all nine railcars around the loop.

```
 ┌────────◄──────────┐
 1  2  3  4  5  6  7  8  9

 ┌────────◄───────┐
 7  6  5  4  3  2  1  8  9

 9  8  1  2  3  4  5  6  7
```

These two moves correctly position railcar 7 which can now be left alone and the next railcar to depart, number 9 be repositioned. The strategy would be to first get railcar 9 to the left hand end and then reverse the order of the eight railcars to the left of railcar 7 to achieve the correct position of railcar 9. In this case railcar 9 is already conveniently at the left hand end so only one move is required and when it is carried out it also carries railcars 8, 1 and 2 into their correct departure positions.

```
 ┌───────◄─────────┐
 9  8  1  2  3  4  5  6  7

 6  5  4  3  2  1  8  9  7
```

The next railcar to position is thus number 4 and this requires two moves

```
 ┌──◄──┐
 6  5  4  3  2  1  8  9  7

 ┌─────◄─────┐
 4  5  6  3  2  1  8  9  7

 3  6  5  4  2  1  8  9  7
```

Again the moves conveniently also place railcar 5 in the right departure position so it only remains to interchange railcars 3 and 6 to achieve the required order

70

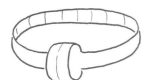

```
  ┌──←┐
  3  6  5  4  2  1  8  9  7

  6  3  5  4  2  1  8  9  ·7
```

In this case the correct departure order has been achieved by 6 moves, where a move is defined as taking a set of railcars around the loop.

11 Paving the patio

							C
A	A	A	A	A	A		C
A					A		C
A		C	C		A	D	C
A		C		A	A		C
A		C					C
A	B	C	C	C	C	C	C
A							

12 Mind stretching

It is possible. The sequence of diagrams indicates how the paper model can be turned inside out and how one can imagine the hole shrinking and the tube returning to its original shape.

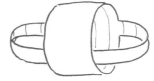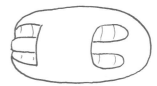

13 The chapel hymnboard

Only 51 cards are necessary.

Because of the possibility of someone choosing the five hymns

    966   699   696   669   666

The 6 (9) digit will have to occur in fifteen different cards.

Because of the possibility of someone choosing five hymns such as

    888   881   882   883   884

all the digits 8, 7, 5, 4, 3, 2, 1 will have to occur on eleven different cards.

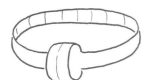

The largest number of occurrences of 0 will be with a selection of hymns such as

100   200   300   400   500

so that 0 will have to occur on ten different cards.

This gives a total of 102 numbers, and by careful pairing of these it will be possible to put them onto 51 cards and satisfy all requirements.

Such a solution would be as follows.

Two cards each of (6, 1) (6, 2) (6, 3) (6, 4) (6, 5) (6, 7) (6, 8)

One card	(6, 0)
Four cards	(0, 8)
Five cards	(8, 7)
Four cards	(7, 5)
Five cards	(5, 4)
Four cards	(4, 3)
Five cards	(3, 2)
Four cards	(2, 1)
Five cards	(1, 0)

14   One step forward, march!

Many solutions are possible with a 4 × 4 board. One is shown here where A → A′, B → B′ etc. The 5 × 5 board however cannot be solved for the simple reason that if there are 13 black squares there will only be 12 white squares, and as a knight jumps from a black square to a white square there are just not enough vacant squares.

D′	A	C′	B
C	B′	D	A′
H′	E	G′	F
G	F′	H	E′

16   Complete the set

The numbers are all of the form n^{10-n} where $n \, \varepsilon \{1, 2, \ldots, 9\}$ so the missing number is $343 = 7^3$.

17   The Old Girls' reunion

Mrs Barbara Brown had duck.
Ms Bridget Baker had roast beef and an ice cream.

This is not such a difficult problem to solve as it may first appear, if tackled systematically using a table.

	Miss Brenda Black	Mrs Barbara Brown	Mrs Beryl Burns	Miss Betty Broad	Ms Bridget Baker
drink	martini	sherry	martini	sherry	fruit juice
meat	steak	duck	r. beef	steak	r. beef
dessert	gateau	ice cream	gateau	fruit salad	ice cream

72

18 The chocolate manufacturer's dilemma

This is a packing problem. By using hexagonal packing instead of square packing the box can hold 50 chocolates instead of 48 and thus be of the correct weight. Instead of 8 rows with 6 chocolates there are 5 rows with 6 chocolates and 4 rows with 5 chocolates. To show that this is a possible solution use circular counters or coins. Theoretically it is not difficult to justify. In square packing the distance between the lines of the centres is $2R$, where R is the radius of the chocolates, whereas in hexagonal packing it is $\sqrt{3}R$, see the diagram. Thus the length of box required for the 9 rows in the hexagonal packing is

Square packing

Hexagonal packing

$$2R + 8\sqrt{3}R \simeq 15.9R$$

which is just less than the $16R$ required by 8 rows in square packing.

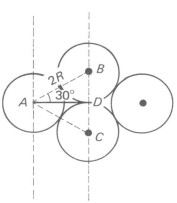

$\triangle ABC$ is equilateral with side $2R$
$AD = 2R\cos 30° = R\sqrt{3}$

19 The Ruby wedding

The Ruby wedding celebration puts the likely ages of William and Ruth above 56, while their ages are not likely to differ by more than one if they shared a desk at school. This suggests numbers which differ by one whose squares differ by a square number.

Now $61^2 - 60^2 = 11^2$
and $85^2 - 84^2 = 13^2$

look likely. The second can be ruled out however as it suggests a family of thirteen children born to a couple who married in their forties. Thus William and 'young Ruth' married when they were 21 and 20 respectively, and raised eleven children.

20 The flight controller's nightmare

No solution is possible.

As soon as flight paths have been arranged from A and B to P, Q and R then one of these airports (P in the diagram) will be inaccessible to flights from C. Eight of the nine flight paths can be planned but not the ninth.

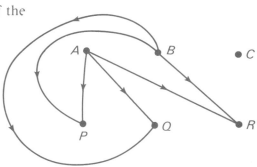

21 Three of a kind

Intelligent use of trial and error starting with possible values for A and deducing possible values for B soon leads to the solution $A = 1$, $B = 4$, $C = 8$. This is the only solution unless you count $A = B = C = 0$.

22 Coin contortions

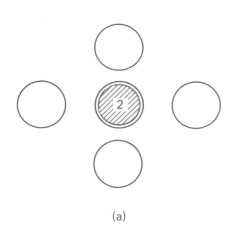

(a)

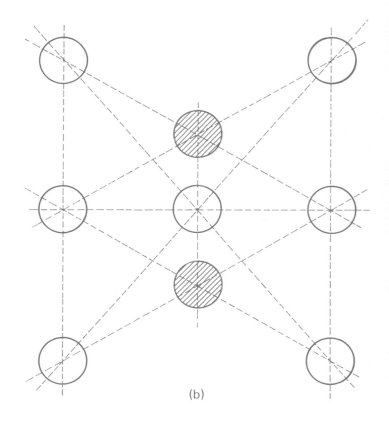

(a) The bottom coin of the cross is moved on top of the centre coin.
(b) The two coins are added to the H pattern to give ten lines of three coins as shown.

(b)

23 An elephantine hole

Take a folded sheet of newspaper and make cuts as shown in the diagram alternately from the folded edge and the edge opposite the fold. Then cut along the fold line from P to Q. The result is a long loop of newspaper. By making a sufficient number of cuts theoretically the loop can be made as large as one pleases and certainly large enough for an elephant!

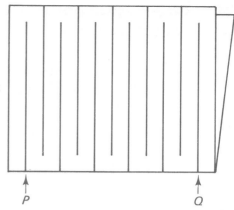

24 Loading the ferry

Using the 'fill each lane from the left' strategy only 11 will be loaded:

left lane $3 + 5 + 9 + 14 + 6 = 37$
middle lane $10 + 11 + 13\quad = 34$
right lane $7 + 8 + 15\qquad = 30.$

This leaves spaces at the ends of the lanes of lengths 3 m, 6 m and 10 m which cannot be utilised by the next vehicle in the queue which is 11 m long. The percentage wastage is thus

$$\frac{(3 + 6 + 10)}{120} \times 100 \simeq 16\%$$

However, by carefully selecting the lane which each vehicle joins as it enters the loading bay it is possible to load 13 vehicles with no wasted space:

3, 5, 9, 14, 6, 10, 11, 13, 7, 8, 15, 11, 8, 4
L L M R R L L R R M M L M

left lane $3 + 5 + 10 + 11 + 11 = 40$
middle lane $9 + 8 + 15 + 8\qquad = 40$
right lane $14 + 6 + 13 + 7\qquad = 40.$

25 Postage due

Using stamps of denominations 2p and 41p *or* 5p and 11p, the largest unobtainable postage would be 39p. Both solutions are correct although the second solution seems more realistic.

26 Ann's tower

The only way Ann could have made exactly three cubes of
bricks from one cube of bricks is if the cubes in the tower
have edges of 5 bricks, 4 bricks and 3 bricks and the box
has an edge equivalent to 6 bricks for

$$3^3 + 4^3 + 5^3 = 6^3$$

and no other reasonably sized numbers satisfy this
relationship.

The tower will be twelve bricks, i.e. 60 cm, high.

28 Reafforestation!

A pegboard and plentiful
supply of pegs would be an
aid to solving this puzzle.
The solution is very satisfying
when you find it because of
its symmetry.

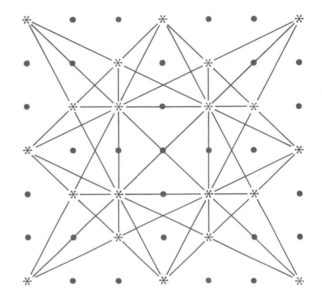

29 Find the route

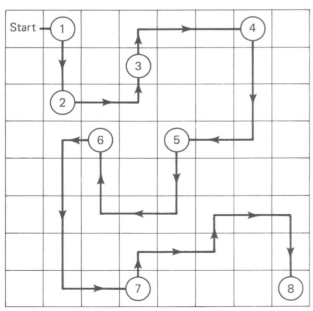

30 The tournament draw

At the end of the first round there need to be 16 (2^4) players left in to allow for a half of the players to be eliminated in each succeeding round. This means that 11 ($27-16$) players have to be eliminated in the first round. This in turn implies 11 first round matches involving 22 players, so only 5 players will receive byes. There will then be 16, 8, 4, 2 players in the succeeding rounds, i.e. 5 rounds altogether.

The number of matches will be half the number of players at each stage so will be

$$11 + 8 + 4 + 2 + 1 = 26.$$

But you could have arrived at this number much more easily. There is only one winner in the competition and 26 losers. Each match determines one loser so for a tournament with N competitors there will need to be precisely $N - 1$ matches to eliminate the $N - 1$ losers.

31 The police officer's beat

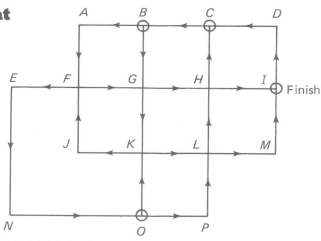

The police officer can patrol the beat by walking 2.6km.

It is impossible to trace out the whole route without retracing at least one street. All possible shortest routes will start and finish at the points O and I and will retrace BC.

One way of doing this is to start at O and follow the route given by

O P L M I D C B G H C B A F E N O K J F G K L H I

which ends at I.

A mathematical analysis of this problem depends on the distribution of odd and even nodes in the network.

33 The stamp machine

Mrs Royale Mail used stamps with values of 1p, 2p, 4p, 8p
and 15p and this solution is based on that of designing the
most efficient set of weights for a pair of scales. In that case
weights of 1, 2, 4, 8 and 16 are used which allows accurate
measurement of weights from 1 to 31. The extra constraint
here was in the coins used which gave the total value of the
stamps as 30p.

A solution where a stamp or connected strip of stamps can
be found to give any value from 1p to 30p takes at least eleven
stamps. The simplest solution is to take a 1p stamp followed
by nine 3p stamps and end with a 2p stamp as shown.

34 Billy Bunter's bargain

He was able to collect 10 free bars.

Using 64 of the 71 labels collected he obtained eight free
bars.

But each of these bars had a label which enabled him to
collect one more free bar. With the label from this bar and
the seven left from the original 71 he could then collect his
tenth bar. Inevitably he had one label from that bar left which
he kept to remind him of his lucky break!

35 All touching

This may seem an impossible problem to solve until you see the solution, (a).

Even more surprising is the ability to arrange seven pencils so that they all touch each other; see (b).

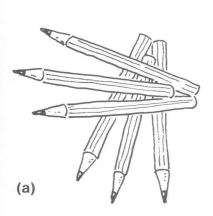

(a)

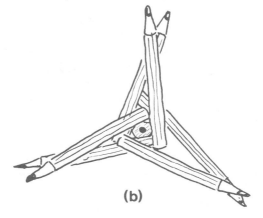

(b)

36   1984 revisited

(*a*) $1985^2 - 1984^2 = 63^2$, an occurrence which last happened in 1860–61.

(*b*) $1984 = 2^{11} - 2^6 = 64(32-1)$ so one solution using eight '4' digits is
$1984 = (4 \times 4 \times 4) \{(4 \times 4 \times \sqrt{4}) - 4/4\}$.
$1984 = (2^8 - 8) \times 8$ so using $[\sqrt{8}]$ which gives the integer part of $\sqrt{8}$ we have $1984 = ([\sqrt{8}]^8 - 8) \times 8$ using just four '8' digits.

37   Identical twins, quads and triplets

$49 \times \quad 101 = 4949$
$38 \times 10101 = 383838$
Now $10101 = 3 \times 7 \times 13 \times 37$

so any 2-digit number *ab* multiplied by 3 then 7 then 13 then 37 will give *ababab*.

$73 \times 101 \times 137 = 1010101$

so the product of *ab* by these numbers produces *abababab*.

38   Rhyme around

Both rhymes are aids to remembering the digits for an approximation to π. Count the number of letters in each word . . .
$\pi = 3.141\ 592\ 653\ 589\ 793\ 238\ 46\ \ldots$

39 Touching coins

(*a*) The usual solution given to this puzzle is to have three coins touching each other in an equilateral triangle array with the fourth coin on top of them. The most satisfying solution is to have the four coins placed as if they are the incircles of the faces of a regular tetrahedron.

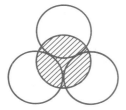 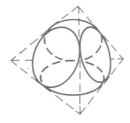

(*b*) A tricky puzzle to solve! First place two coins touching each other flat on top of a third coin as shown. Now stand two coins on the bottom coin and tilt them, to touch each other. With care the 'standing' coins can be placed to touch all three horizontal coins thus solving the problem.

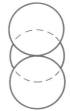 

40 Two wrongs make a right

This is just one of the hundreds of puzzles set by the Victorian king of puzzles Henry Ernest Dudeney. It has more than one solution. Four are given here

$$
\begin{array}{r}
25938 \\
+\ 25938 \\
\hline
51876
\end{array}
\qquad
\begin{array}{r}
25387 \\
+\ 25387 \\
\hline
50764
\end{array}
\qquad
\begin{array}{r}
25469 \\
+\ 25469 \\
\hline
50938
\end{array}
\qquad
\begin{array}{r}
49265 \\
+\ 49265 \\
\hline
98530
\end{array}
$$

41 Narcissistic numbers

$371 = 3^3 + 7^3 + 1^3$
$407 = 4^3 + 0^3 + 7^3$

42 Inside and out

The fact is the hoops can be anywhere as long as the four smaller hoops do not overlap each other. The area inside a circle of radius 50 cm is 2500π cm^2. The total area inside the four circles of radius 40 cm, 20 cm, 20 cm and 10 cm is

$$(1600\pi + 400\pi + 400\pi + 100\pi) = 2500\pi \text{ cm}^2$$

which is identical to the large circle. Start with all of the smaller hoops outside the large hoop, when the shaded areas clearly balance. Now imagine the 40 cm radius hoop moving towards the large hoop and overlapping it. The overlapping area is then lost to the 40 cm hoop and is also lost to the large hoop, so the balance of the shaded areas is maintained. The same argument applies if the other hoops overlap the large one so there is no difficulty in obtaining a balance!

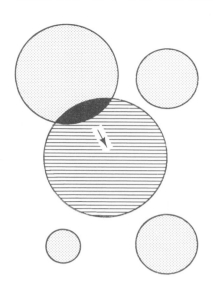

43 Matchstick manoeuvres

Four matches have to be moved so the number of matches in the solution is twelve, the same as at the start.

As three identical squares are to be formed we are looking for three squares with no matchstick common to two squares. From the starting point, five solutions at first seem possible, see below, but only the last three are solutions as the others require that more than four matches are moved. It is also possible to form three identical squares by moving only three matches. Can you see how?

44 Micro millions

$$1\,000\,000\,000 = 10^9 = 2^9 \times 5^9$$
$$= 512 \times 1\,953\,125$$

Any other factorisation will involve $2 \times 5 = 10$ and so involve a zero digit. With the usual price of micros being in hundreds of pounds the conclusion is that $1\,953\,125$ micros were sold at £512.

A related investigation is to see which powers of 10 can be expressed as the product of two factors, neither of which contains a zero digit. 10^{10} cannot be so expressed, for example, as $2^{10} = 1024$.

45 The economy cut

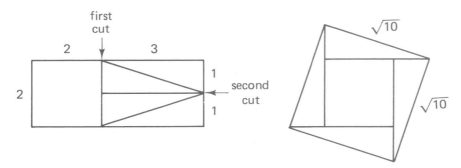

Feel pleased if you managed it with four cuts but congratulate yourself if you managed it in three cuts like Emma.

She first cut off a 2×2 square then cut the remaining rectangle into two 3×1 rectangles. Next she superimposed one of these rectangles on the other and cut along a diagonal to give herself four identical triangles which fitted neatly around the 2×2 square to form a $\sqrt{10} \times \sqrt{10}$ square. No doubt she lost some size in sewing the pieces together but the square she obtained would cover her 3×3 table.

46 The variable menu

420 days pass before a meal is repeated.

The potato cycle is 4 long, the meat cycle 5 long, the vegetable cycle 7 long and the sweet cycle 3 long. Thus the first time the first meal can repeat is after $4 \times 5 \times 7 \times 3$ days, i.e. on the 421st day which is well into the second year.

As 100 is a multiple of 4 and 5 then rice and beef will be served on day 100. Further, as 100 leaves a remainder of 2 on division by 7, and a remainder of 1 on division by 3 the rest of the meal will consist of carrots and apple pie.

To find when roast potatoes, lamb, sprouts and apple pie are served we need to find the smallest number that

leaves a remainder of 3 on division by 4
leaves a remainder of 2 on division by 5
leaves a remainder of 6 on division by 7
leaves a remainder of 1 on division by 3.

The answer is 307.

Adding sausages and turnips to the meat and vegetable columns makes the four cycles of lengths 4, 6, 8 and 3 with an LCM of 24 so the meals repeat themselves every 24 days.

47 Not in her prime

$$2 \times 7 \times 13 \times 97 = 17654$$

The only plausible deduction is that the computer programmer was 26, her cat was 7 and her house number 97.

48 Loop-line limitations

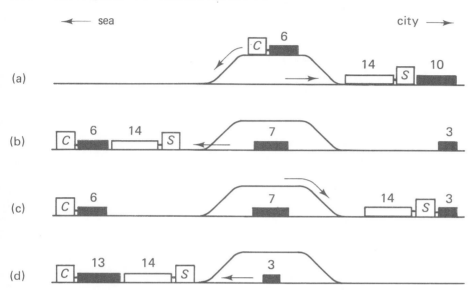

The train from the city, C, uncouples 10 carriages and takes 6 carriages onto the loop. The train arriving from the seaside, S, stays on the branch line and pulls up to the 10 carriages left by the city train. See (a). The train, C, on the loop now travels onto the branch line with its 6 carriages while train S pulls 7 of the seaside bound carriages along the branch line and leaves them between the points while continuing with its own 14 carriages until it is outside the points. See (b).

Train S now travels around the loop, and couples up with the remaining 3 seaside bound carriages. See (c). S reverses back along the branch line leaving the 3 seaside bound carriages between the points, and in the meantime C has reversed and picked up its 7 carriages. See (d). It is now a simple matter for train S to travel around the loop and to the city, leaving train C to reverse along the branch line to pick up its remaining 3 carriages before setting off for the seaside.

49 As easy as abc!

$$2^5 \times 9^2 = 2592$$

50 Magic polygons

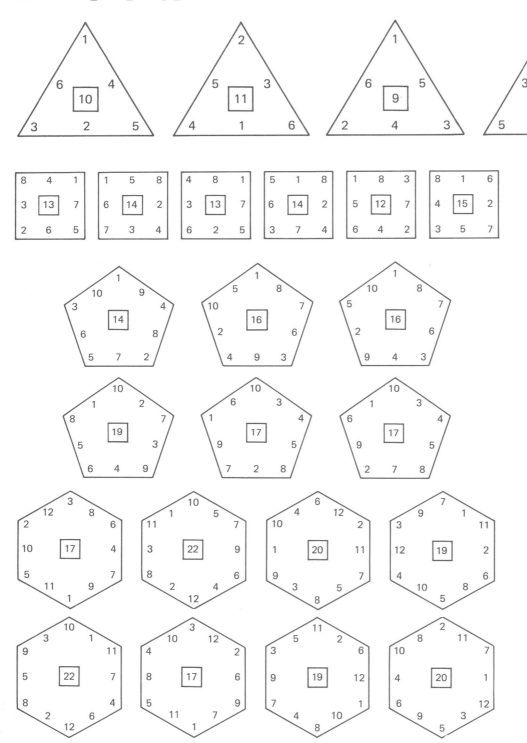

The first polygon of each kind above corresponds to the
solution of that in the puzzle.

84

A close look at the solutions given will show that they are related in pairs. Take all the numbers in one of the square solutions away from 9 and it gives one of the other square solutions. The number 9 is chosen as it is 1 more than the largest number used in the square solutions. Thus once you have a new solution the transformation $n \rightarrow 9 - n$ gives another.

Similarly $n \rightarrow 11 - n$ and $n \rightarrow 12 - n$ will generate further solutions for the pentagon and hexagon respectively.

When trying to find a solution to a magic polygon it is helpful to decide first on a magic sum. But what numbers are possible for such a sum? Consider the hexagon which contains the numbers 1 to 12.

Six times the magic sum, S, must be the total of the numbers 1 to 12 (equal to 78) added to the total of the numbers at the vertices, as these each occur on two sides. The smallest corner total is $1+2+3+4+5+6 = 21$ and the largest is $7+8+9+10+11+12 = 57$ so it follows that

$$99 \leqslant 6S \leqslant 135$$

from which

$$S = 17, 18, 19, 20, 21 \text{ or } 22.$$

Suppose you decide to try 17 as a magic sum. The next thing to do is to look systematically at all the sets of three numbers from 1 to 12 which sum to 17:

12+4+1	12+3+2	11+5+1	11+4+2	10+6+1
10+5+2	10+4+3	9+7+1	9+6+2	9+5+3
8+7+2	8+6+3	8+5+4	7+6+4	

Then it is helpful to note how often each number occurs in a set. For example, 12 only occurs twice so it is advisable to put this into the hexagon first and then in the middle of a side where it will not be needed again. These strategies narrow down the field but trial and error and patience are still required. With experience further strategies recommend themselves but the above should give you a good start.

51 Factors galore

Any such number must be a multiple of the LCM of $1, 2, \dots$ 18, that is 12 252 240, and this gives a practical approach to finding all the solutions which are

$$2\,438\,195\,760 = 12\,252\,240 \times 199$$
$$3\,785\,942\,160 = 12\,252\,240 \times 309$$
$$4\,753\,869\,120 = 12\,252\,240 \times 388$$
$$4\,876\,391\,520 = 12\,252\,240 \times 398$$

52 Fascinating fractions

The solutions are not necessarily unique as the following show.

$$\frac{1}{2} = \frac{7\,293}{14\,586} = \frac{6\,729}{13\,458} = \frac{7269}{14\,538}$$

$$\frac{1}{3} = \frac{5\,823}{17\,469} = \frac{5\,832}{17\,496}$$

$$\frac{1}{4} = \frac{7\,956}{31\,824} = \frac{5\,796}{23\,184} = \frac{3\,942}{15\,768} = \frac{4\,392}{17\,568}$$

$$\frac{1}{5} = \frac{2\,697}{13\,485}$$

$$\frac{1}{6} = \frac{2\,943}{17\,658} = \frac{4\,653}{27\,918} = \frac{5\,697}{34\,182}$$

$$\frac{1}{7} = \frac{2\,394}{16\,758} = \frac{2\,637}{18\,459} = \frac{4\,527}{31\,689}$$

$$\frac{1}{8} = \frac{3\,187}{25\,496} = \frac{4\,589}{36\,712} = \frac{4\,591}{36\,728} = \frac{6\,789}{54\,312}$$

$$\frac{1}{9} = \frac{6\,381}{57\,429} = \frac{6\,471}{58\,239}$$

53 How large a number can you make?

This is an interesting investigation in the use of notation and then in deciding which numbers are the largest.

2^{31} and 3^{21} are both large but which is the larger?

Now $\dfrac{2^{31}}{3^{21}} = 2^{10}\left(\dfrac{2}{3}\right)^{21} = 2^{10}\left(\dfrac{4}{9}\right)^{10}\dfrac{2}{3} = \left(\dfrac{8}{9}\right)^{10}\dfrac{2}{3} < 1$

so $\quad 2^{31} < 3^{21}$

When the factorial notation is used then the numbers can become enormous. Some of these are shown below in order of size.

$$321! < (2^{31})! < (3^{21})! < 3^{21!} < 2^{31!} < .1^{-(32!)}$$

The justification of this order is very interesting and shows how different the numbers are. For example

$$321! << 321^{321} < (3^6)^{321} = 3^{1926} << 3^{21!}$$

$.1^{-(32!)}$ which is equivalent to 1 followed by 32! zeros is the largest found by the author.

54 Food for thought

The first row is easy to complete, but then anyone trying an empirical approach will almost always try integers and not be able to complete the square. The point is that the magic total is always three times the number in the centre of the square. Using this fact leads to the number in the centre as being $6\frac{2}{3}$ and the rest follows.

11	3	6
$1\frac{2}{3}$	$6\frac{2}{3}$	$11\frac{2}{3}$
$7\frac{1}{3}$	$10\frac{1}{3}$	$2\frac{1}{3}$

55 How many will you take?

A player, to win, must leave his opponent eventually with 1 counter. To do this, at his penultimate move, he must leave 5 counters, for if he leaves 2, 3 or 4 counters his opponent could always take away 1, 2 or 3 counters to leave one. On the other hand, if he left 6, 7 or 8 counters his opponent could leave him with 5 and a losing position.

A similar line of reasoning shows that it is 'safe' to leave totals of 9, 13, 17, 21, . . ., $4n + 1$, for no matter what his opponent's play is from one of these totals he can always play to leave the next smaller pile in the sequence . . . until his opponent is faced with removing the last counter.

The player knowing this underlying strategy will normally beat his opponent for if he finds himself starting with an 'unsafe' total such as 19 counters he can remove 2 counters to leave a 'safe' total and be sure of winning if from then on he arranges his play to complement his opponent's so that they jointly remove 4 counters at each stage.

56 The dishonest gold exporter

The customs officer weighed together 1 ingot from the first pile, 2 ingots from the second pile, 3 ingots from the third pile, ..., 10 ingots from the tenth pile. Altogether 55 ingots whose legal weight is known. If the fourth pile contains the light ingots then the total weight of the 55 ingots will be 4 g below their legal weight. The number of grams below the legal weight will always indicate which is the pile of fraudulent ingots in a consignment. A neat solution!

58 Ten Tors training

The shortest route takes
16.6 miles.

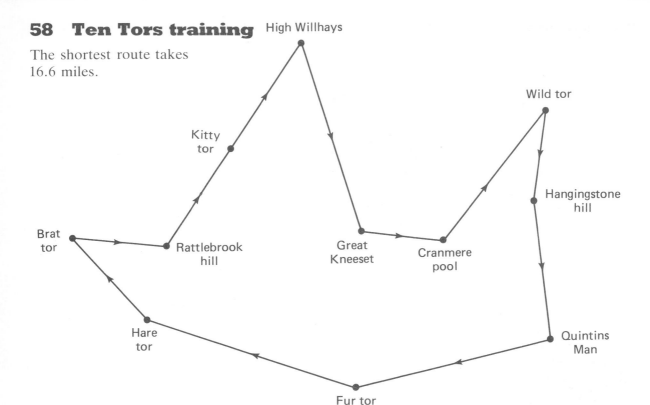

59 Alphametic puzzles

CRAM and COE have several outcomes:

$$
\begin{array}{r} 7850 \\ +\ 72E \\ \hline 857E \end{array}
\qquad
\begin{array}{r} 5610 \\ +\ 54E \\ \hline 615E \end{array}
\qquad
\begin{array}{r} 8970 \\ +\ 81E \\ \hline 978E \end{array}
$$

$E = 1, 3, 4, 6, 9$ $E = 2, 3, 7, 8, 9$ $E = 2, 3, 4, 5, 6$

but if $E = 1, 5, 7$ or 8 the solution is unique.

Two solutions for SANTA are

$$
\begin{array}{r} 24794 \\ -\ 16452 \\ \hline 8342 \end{array}
\qquad \text{and} \qquad
\begin{array}{r} 36156 \\ -\ 28693 \\ \hline 7463 \end{array}
$$

With the slogan for MARS several solutions are possible.
For example when $M = 0$, $A = 2$, $R = 5$, $S = 6$, $E = 7$ and $T = 9$, then B can be any one of $1, 3, 4$ or 8.

88

60 K9 or One man and his dog

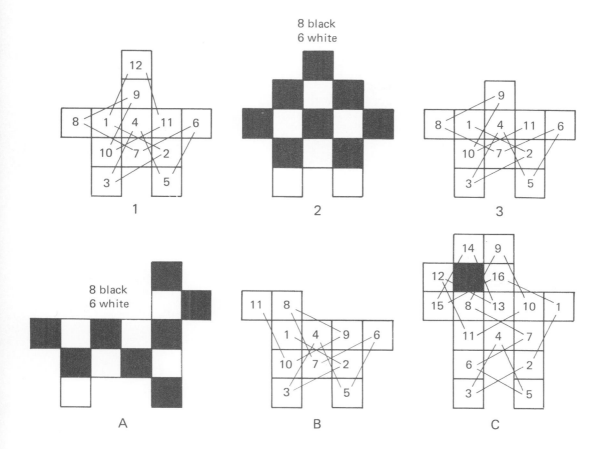

If the squares are shaded alternately black and white the knight must always move to a square of a different colour. Hence a re-entrant tour is only possible if there are an equal number of black and white squares. If there is one more black than white square a tour is also possible but there is no possible tour if there are 2 more black squares than white.

So 1 pairs with C, 2 pairs with A and 3 pairs with B.

62 Topsy-turvy

If $abc \ldots k \times 9 = k \ldots cba$ then it is easy to see that $a = 1$ and $k = 9$, for any other value of a would lead to a number being carried, and hence generating a number involving more digits than the original.

But $19 \times 9 \neq 91$ because of the 8 to be carried when multiplying the 9 in the units column by 9.

Consideration of $1b9 \times 9$ soon shows that it cannot be equal to $9b1$ again because of the carry over.

However, consideration of

$$1\,b\,c\,9 \times 9 = 9\,c\,b\,1$$

soon leads to the fact that $b = 0$ and then $c = 8$ satisfies the given requirements.

$$1089 \times 9 = 9801$$

This is the smallest solution, and the only one with 4 digits. The next three solutions are

10 989	5 digits
109 989	6 digits
1 099 989	7 digits.

Then, with an obvious pattern emerging, there are two solutions with 8 digits, namely

$$10\ 999\ 989 \quad \text{and} \quad 10\ 891\ 089.$$

and again with 9 digits:

$$109\ 999\ 989 \quad \text{and} \quad 108\ 901\ 089.$$

With 10 digits three solutions are possible

$$1\ 099\ 999\ 989 \quad 1\ 089\ 001\ 089 \quad 1\ 098\ 910\ 989$$

but these build on existing solutions and no new principle is required to find the solutions with any number of digits.

The numbers whose digits are reversed by multiplying by 4 are closely related to the above – in fact are all double the above.

$$1\ 089 \times 2 = 2\ 178 \quad \text{and} \quad 2\ 178 \times 4 = 8\ 712$$
$$10\ 989 \times 2 = 21\ 978 \quad \text{and} \quad 21\ 978 \times 4 = 87\ 912$$

and so on.

63   Which was the winning strategy?

Bruce and Christine tie for first place, followed by Daphne, and then Alan. To see why this is so imagine the race to be 16 km long.

Alan takes $1\frac{1}{2}$ hours, for 8 km at 16 km/h takes $\frac{1}{2}$ hour and 8 km at 8 km/h takes an hour.

Bruce takes $1\frac{1}{3}$ hours. Suppose his time is t hours then from the fact that half of this time is spent at 16 km/h and half at 8 km/h we have

$$(\tfrac{1}{2}t \times 16) + (\tfrac{1}{2}t \times 8) = 16$$

from which $12t = 16$ so $t = 1\frac{1}{3}$

Christine running at a steady 12 km/h also takes *1 $\frac{1}{3}$ hours*.

Daphne runs the same number of paces at both speeds but experience shows

(*a*) that the length of pace at the higher speed is longer than at the slower speed so she will run more than half the distance at the higher speed and thus take less time than Alan.

(*b*) the time taken for a pace at the higher speed will be less than the time taken for a pace at the lower speed so she will spend more than half of her time at the slower speed and consequently take longer than Bruce.

64 A topological trick

First Nuala takes her string at about its middle and passes it under the loop of string around Norman's right wrist, *A*, on the inside of the wrist and in the direction from elbow to hand. Next she loops the string up over his hand to the outside of his wrist. She should now be able to walk away leaving Norman and any onlookers amazed. Their own wrists will still be tied together but they will not be linked together. Be warned, however, if you don't follow the instructions precisely the strings can easily become more entwined.

For example, if Nuala's string goes from *Q* under Norman's string before looping around it to *P*, then Nuala will need to operate on Norman's left wrist as above instead of his right wrist. The only way to appreciate how this works is to do it with a friend, as many times and as slowly as it requires to follow what happens.

65 The blanket box

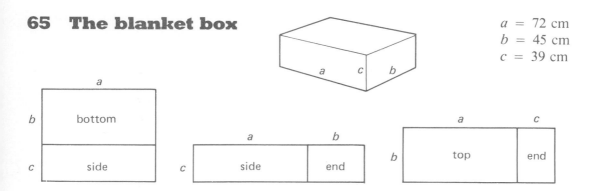

$a = 72$ cm
$b = 45$ cm
$c = 39$ cm

The dimensions may be found by trial and error but can be approached analytically as follows.

Let the dimensions be a, b, c as shown and let the areas of the three pieces of plywood be X, Y and Z respectively, then

$$X = ab + ac \qquad Y = ac + bc \qquad Z = ab + bc$$

so $\quad \frac{1}{2}(X + Y - Z) = ac \quad \frac{1}{2}(Y + Z - X) = bc \quad \frac{1}{2}(Z + X - Y) = ab$

Use $\frac{ac.bc}{ab}$ to find c and then the other two dimensions are easily determined.

66 Divisibility

Use divisibility tests. The 5, for example, must be in the middle, for no other five-digit number constructed from the digits 1, 2, . . ., 9 is divisible by 5. As all the digits sum to 45, and this is divisible by 9, any order for the digits will always be divisible by 9 so divisibility by 9 can be taken for granted. The sum of the first six digits must be divisible by 3 and the sixth digit must be even for the number formed from the first six digits to be divisible by 6. In fact every other digit must be even for the required divisibility by 2, 4, 6 and 8.

Such arguments as the foregoing help considerably, but use of the calculator and a certain amount of trial and error will be required to find the number divisible by 7.

There is only one solution: 381 654 729.

But be warned of too much dependence on your calculator. If it only displays 8 digits then 963 258 147 will appear to be a solution for it will appear that 96 325 814 is divisible by 8 . . . but this is impossible as 814 does not divide by 8.

67 Calculator challenge

$2025 = 45^2 \qquad 3136 = 56^2$
$2025 + 1111 = 3136$ and further $45 + 11 = 56$.

68 Toasting efficiently

Let the three slices of bread be A, B, C with sides $a_1, a_2, b_1, b_2, c_1,$ and c_2. Then the minimum time to toast the three slices on both sides is 107 seconds.

Time in seconds						
1–3	insert A	↑				
4–6	insert B	a_1	↑			
34–35	turn A	↓	b_1			
37–39	remove B	↑	↓			
40–42	insert C	a_2		↑		
66–68	remove A	↓		c_1		
69–71	insert B		↑	↓		
73–74	turn C		b_2	↑		
102–104	remove B		↓	c_2		
105–107	remove C			↓		

69 Playing safe!

3 will do.

70 Odds on winning

Place £95 as follows:

> £35 on Brigadoon so that at 2 to 1, should he win, you would collect £105.
>
> £30 on Tophatter so that at 5 to 2, should he win, you would collect £105.
>
> £15 each on Lightning and Virginsky so that at 6 to 1, should either win, you would again collect £105 and thus be certain of gaining £10.

It is a rare occasion in reality for the odds to be balanced so that a punter could be certain of winning as in this case. To see when it is possible find the sum of the reciprocals of the odds plus 1. (Where the odds are of the form m to n they must first be reduced to the form m/n to 1). When the total of the reciprocals is less than 1 you are onto a winner.

With the race discussed:

> odds of 2 to 1 correspond to $1/(2+1) = \frac{1}{3}$;
> odds of 5 to 2 are equal to 2.5 to 1 which correspond to $1/3.5 = \frac{2}{7}$
> odds of 6 to 1 correspond to $\frac{1}{7}$

so the sum of the reciprocals is

$$\frac{1}{3} + \frac{2}{7} + \frac{1}{7} + \frac{1}{7} = \frac{7}{21} + \frac{6}{21} + \frac{3}{21} + \frac{3}{21} = \frac{19}{21} < 1$$

from which it can be deduced that for a stake of £19 it would be possible to win back £2 by staking

> £7 on Brigadoon, £6 on Tophatter, and £3 each on Lightning and Virginsky.

71 Tangrams

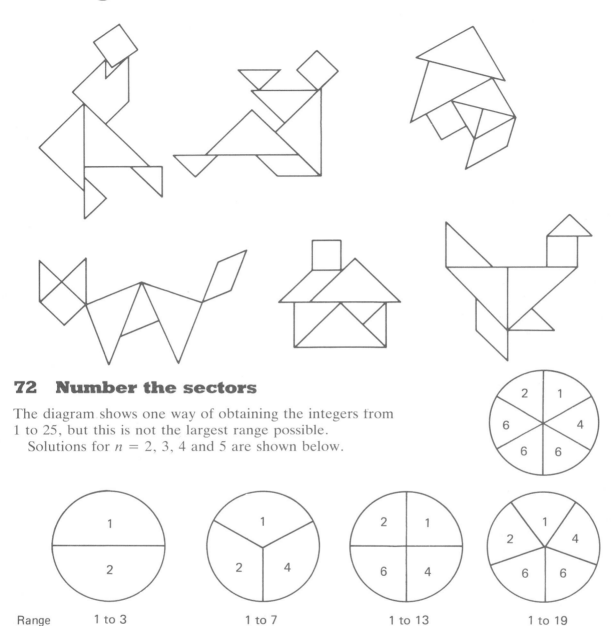

72 Number the sectors

The diagram shows one way of obtaining the integers from 1 to 25, but this is not the largest range possible.

Solutions for $n = 2, 3, 4$ and 5 are shown below.

| Range | 1 to 3 | 1 to 7 | 1 to 13 | 1 to 19 |

It is very tempting to extrapolate from these solutions and assume that the optimum range is achieved by having the sectors numbered

$$1, 2, 6, 6, \ldots, 6, 4$$

when the number of sectors is four or more, but this is not the case. With six sectors the sequence

$$1, 2, 5, 9, 6, 4 \quad \text{gives 1 to 27.}$$

73 Rearranging the hospital ward

Two screens are sufficient as shown in the adjacent diagram.

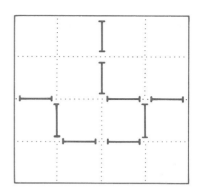

74 One hundred up!

To work out a winning strategy start with the end point 100. If you can call 89 your opponent cannot reach 100 in his next turn but must put you in range of a win. So how can you put yourself in a position to call 89? If you go back 11 to 78 the same argument holds. Call 78 and your opponent must put you in range of 89 without being able to get there. So how can you put yourself in a position to call 78? The answer of course is to go back 11 to 67 … and then back 11 to 56 and so on.

The critical sequence is thus

1, 12, 23, 34, 45, 56, 67, 78, 89.

As soon as your opponent makes a call which is not in this sequence you will be able to call one of these numbers and then follow the sequence home to 100. Unless your opponent is aware of this strategy your chances of winning must be very high.

75 Hidden shapes

(a) This should not present too many problems. The halves of A are isosceles trapeziums equivalent to the shape obtained by cutting a regular hexagon in half by a diagonal joining opposite vertices. The solutions are shown below together with some further shapes. Recording these shapes is best done on isometric paper.

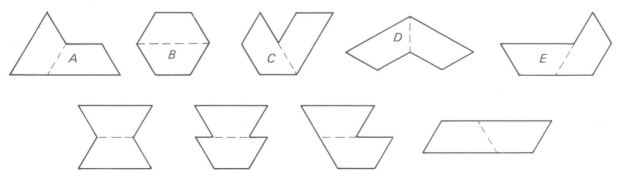

(*b*) The division of *A* into four shapes similar to *A* is shown in
     (i). Other shapes which can be divided into four equal
     similar shapes are easier to find than one first imagines.
     Any parallelogram or triangle can be so divided and so,
     for example, can the L shape and the half hexagon shown
     in (ii).

(i)

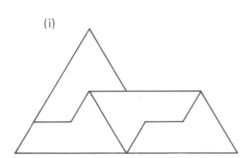

(ii)

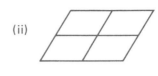

(*c*) Note the change in wording. Equal areas are required
     this time, not equal shapes.

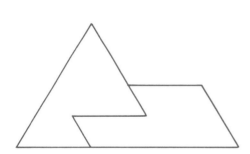

76   Always one short

59 is the smallest number.

The key to this activity is to realise that any number which
is 1 less than a number which has 6, 5, 4, 3 and 2 as factors will
have the required property. The smallest such number will
thus be 1 less than the LCM of 6, 5, 4, 3 and 2. Further, any
number of the form $(60n - 1)$ will have the same property.

The same argument applies to the last part:

$$\text{LCM} \{10, 9, 8, 7, 6, 5, 4, 3, 2\} = 2520$$

so any number of the form $2520n - 1$ is a solution.

In particular the three less than 10 000 are 2519, 5039,
7559.

77 Amoeboid patterns

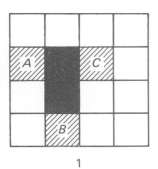

1

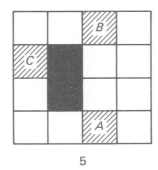

5

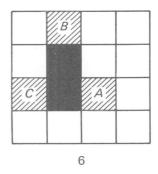

6

Each shape is made up of five squares, two of which do not move. The three other squares, A, B and C, however, slide around the two fixed squares in an anticlockwise direction, one square at a time. Shapes 5 and 6 are shown above. By considering each of A, B and C in turn it can be seen that they return to their original position after 10 moves, so shape 11 will be identical to shape 1.

The second amoeboid pattern has one fixed square while two of the other squares move together as a 2×1 rectangle. As before, the squares A and B, and rectangle C slide around the fixed square in an anticlockwise direction. However, whereas A or B would be able to circumnavigate the fixed square in 8 moves, if unimpeded, it takes the rectangle 10 moves.

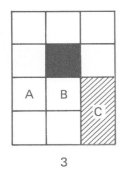

3

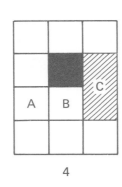

4

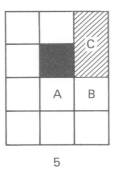

5

The result is that from time to time the squares A and B have to remain still while the rectangle C moves out of their path. This happens from shape 3 to shape 4 in the given sequence.

How many steps are required to get back to the original shape?

78 The Embassy reception

Each ambassador shakes the hands of 79 other ambassadors. There are 80 ambassadors but each handshake involves two people which gives

$$(80 \times 79) \div 2 = 3160 \text{ handshakes.}$$

79 Quartering a circle

Symmetric solutions, where the quarters are identical in shape as well as area, are not too difficult to come by, but unsymmetric solutions are not easy to produce accurately.

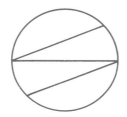
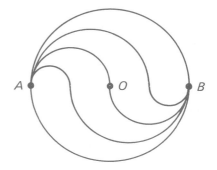

The solution using three curves of equal lengths based on semicircles of ¾, ½, and ¼ the diameter of the original circle is very satisfying.

80 Sweeping the park efficiently

The worker can't sweep the paths without retracing some of them. The shortest distance which he can travel is 1560m (1330m for the total length of the pathway plus 230m for the paths retraced). This is achieved by retracing AB, HG and IF and there are many different routes which give the shortest distance. An example of one is:

H B C D H I D E F I F G H G A B A H

A mathematical analysis of this problem depends on the distribution of odd and even nodes in the network.

81   Pentomino Parcels

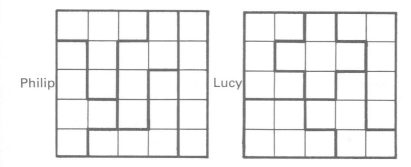

Philip

Lucy

The two hampers are as shown.

Philip has: a coat, a camera, a train set, books, and a
fishing rod.

Lucy has: a stool, a clock, a hockey stick, shoes, and a
cycle.

82   A stamp book with a difference

The impossible total is 18p. The 7p, 9p and 2p stamps total
18p but are not connected by their edges in the book. The
question of what is the limiting value for N arises and one
way of looking for a limit is to find how many ways a stamp
or set of connected stamps can be removed from the 2×3
array.

There are 40 possible ways of removing stamps so this sets
an upper limit to N, however the constraints of the problem
limit the maximum value of N to 36. This can be achieved
in the two ways shown below. Check in each case that 1p to
36p are all attainable.

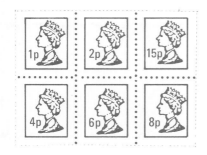

83 Some curious number relations

Further examples are

$$63 = 6^2 + 3^3$$
$$175 = 1^1 + 7^2 + 5^3$$
$$598 = 5^1 + 9^2 + 8^3$$
$$1306 = 1^1 + 3^2 + 0^3 + 6^4$$
$$1676 = 1^1 + 6^2 + 7^3 + 6^4.$$

Another most unusual relationship is

$$4^4 + 3^3 + 8^8 + 5^5 + 7^7 + 9^9 + 0^0 + 8^8 + 8^8 = 438\,579\,088$$

84 Concentric magic squares

The number in the centre cell is 13 which is the middle number in 1 to 25.

The 3×3 square has a magic total of $39\,(=3 \times 13)$ and the 5×5 square has a magic total of $65 = (5 \times 13)$.

Similar rules apply to the 9×9 magic square and the squares inside it whose magic totals are all multiples of 41. So the 3×3 square has a magic total of $205 = 41 \times 5$, the 7×7 square has a magic total of $287 = 41 \times 7$ and the 9×9 square has a magic total of 369.

An excellent reference on magic squares is

Magic Squares and Cubes by W.S. Andrews (Dover)

11	2	25	18	9
10	12	21	6	16
4	7	13	19	22
23	20	5	14	3
17	24	1	8	15

85 Connecting the fire hydrants

The minimum length of water main is 520m.
Join ABHGIEF then add in CI and DI.

86 To set you thinking

It is important to appreciate that the question does not ask for three *identical* equilateral triangles. A satisfying puzzle to solve.

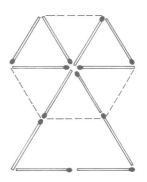

87 Kirkman's schoolgirls problem

day 1	day 2	day 3	day 4
195	296	397	498
278	381	412	523
346	457	568	671

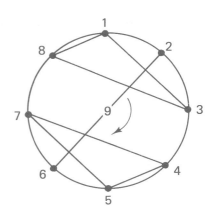

One solution to the 9 schoolboys problem is shown here together with a neat geometric representation of it.

9 is placed at the centre of a circle and the numbers $1, 2, \ldots,$ 8 are placed symmetrically around its circumference. A diameter and two triangles are drawn as shown which group the nine digits into three triplets. These correspond to day 2 of the solution given.

Now imagine the diameter and triangles rotating about the centre of the circle through 45° clockwise. They now group the nine digits into three completely different triplets. Repeated rotations of 45° generate four distinct sets of triplets which correspond to the solution given. Clearly by changing the order of the numbers on the circle many other solutions can easily be found.

The original Kirkman's schoolgirls problem is much harder to solve but a solution can be expressed using a circle and triangles as shown here, where repeated rotations of a seventh of a revolution are required to give the different form of the crocodile on consecutive days.

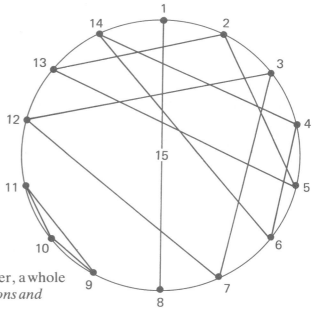

The position of the triangles shown corresponds to the crocodile

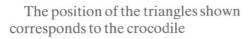

$(1, 15, 8),\ (2, 5, 13),\ (3, 7, 12),$
$(4, 6, 14),\ (9, 10, 11)$

and following days can be found by leaving 15 untouched and adding 2 to all the other numbers where the addition is such that $14 + 2 = 2, 13 + 2 = 1$.

For anyone wishing to pursue this puzzle further, a whole chapter is devoted to it in *Mathematical Recreations and Essays* by W.W. Rouse Ball.

88 Spot the pattern

The colour of a circle is determined by the two circles immediately above and left and right of it. If the two upper circles are the same colour, then the lower circle is white, if different the lower circle is black.

Each row of circles is to be thought of as a continuous band so that the circle at the right hand end is followed by (or next to) the circle at the left hand end.

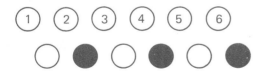

Thus in deciding the colour of the last circle in a new row, it has to be seen as below the first and last circles of the previous row. After the first row the number of black circles (and of white circles) must be even. Why?

An all white row can only follow from an all white row or an all black row. So it depends on the possibility of an all black row. Now an all black row can only be obtained from a row which alternates white and black and this can be shown to be unobtainable as the following argument shows.

Suppose 6 is white, then 1 must be black to give the black circle on the right hand end. Then 2 must be black also for 1 and 2 to give the white on the left hand end. 2 black implies 3 white, which in turn implies 4 white, which in turn implies 5 black. But this makes 5 and 6 of opposite colours which contradict with the fact that the penultimate circle is white. Clearly a similar contradiction would have arisen if we started by letting 6 be black.

A single black circle is also impossible for it would have to arise from a black circle and a white circle and a little thought will soon show that at least one more black circle must occur.

The pattern must repeat itself at some stage for there is only a finite number of possible patterns for a row and the process goes on generating new rows ad infinitum!

89   Two of a kind

8	1	6
3	5	7
4	9	2

XMAS	RUM	HOME
BABY	TURKEYS	HOLLY
CANDLE	CRIB	SOCK

Both games are structurally the same as Os and Xs. The only way *three* numbers from 1 to 9 can total 15 is if they form either a row, or a column, or a diagonal of the above magic square.

The nine words have been chosen so that when they are put in the above 3×3 array, *three* words will only have a letter in common if they form a row, a column, or a diagonal.

90   Carving up the camels

Perhaps deathbeds aren't the best place for mental arithmetic! The shares the elderly arab allocated to his sons do not add up to 1.

$$\frac{1}{2}+\frac{1}{3}+\frac{1}{8}=\frac{23}{24}$$

By the uncle's solution in fact they all gained.

Ahab receives $\frac{12}{23}>\frac{1}{2}$

Aziz receives $\frac{8}{23}>\frac{1}{3}$

Abdul receives $\frac{3}{23}>\frac{1}{8}$

This is a very old puzzle but well worth repeating.

91 Thwaites' conjecture

Trying to predict the length of the sequence from a given start number has so far been found impossible in general. For example, 27 takes 111 stages to reach 1, but who would have guessed? However, 2^n converges to 1 in n stages and is very predictable, e.g. $32 \rightarrow 16 \rightarrow 8 \rightarrow 4 \rightarrow 2 \rightarrow 1$.

This process is easy to program on a micro and facilitates the investigation. Further, it allows comparison with other similar processes such as computing $3N + 5$ or $5N - 13$ when N is odd.

92 A fascinating family of square numbers

Consider any number in the sequence, say, 11 115 556

$$11\,115\,556 \times 9 = 100\,040\,004 = 10002^2$$

It is easier to see the underlying pattern, and how it will continue for all numbers in the sequence if we look at

$$
\begin{aligned}
11\,115\,556 \times (10 - 1) = \quad & 111\,155\,560 \\
- \quad & \underline{11\,115\,556} \\
& 100\,040\,004
\end{aligned}
$$

Clearly numbers of the form 1000...4000...4 are square. Now we got this number from the original number in the sequence by multiplying that number by 9, itself a square number, so that too must be square.

The only other similar sequence is produced by expanding 49 by repeatedly introducing 48.

     49   4489   444 889   44 448 889   etc.

In this case $444\,889 \times 9 = 4\,004\,001 = 2001^2$, for example, showing how closely related the two sets of numbers are.

93 Playing detective

$$2 \times 7 \times 23 \times 59 = 18\,998$$

The only plausible deduction from what we already know about the teacher is that the size of her class is 23, her telephone bill is £118, she had four sons and three daughters.

94 Community coppers

Ten police are required for the problem given and can be arranged as shown.

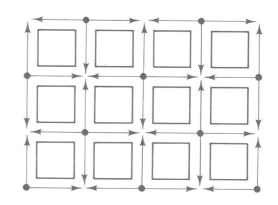

95 The shunting yard

Uncouple the trucks between 11 and 12 and use the engine to shunt 10 and 11 onto b. Return the engine with 1 to 9 to c.

Uncouple the trucks between 7 and 8 and use the engine to shunt 7 onto b. Return the engine with 1 to 6 to c.

Uncouple the trucks between 3 and 4 and then use the engine to shunt trucks 1 to 3 to b and couple 3 to 7 and 7 to 10.

    Shunt trucks 3, 7, 10 to a and return with 1 and 2 to c.

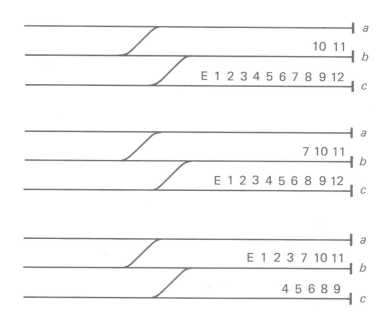

96 A symmetric cross-number puzzle

The symmetry about the two lines at 45° automatically generates all the symmetry of a square so by the time all the black squares are filled in there are only a limited number of spaces to be filled. Because of the symmetry required the 2-digit number around the central square must be of the form xx, and to be prime must be 11. Similarly it can be argued that the number bordering each edge must be of the form $xyyx$.

    Such a number must have 11 as a factor so cannot be prime. It must therefore be $11^3 = 1331$.

The remaining squares require pairs of numbers of the form xy and yx which are both prime such as 13 and 31, 17 and 71, and 37 and 73.

One solution is shown and three others are possible using the alternative corners given.

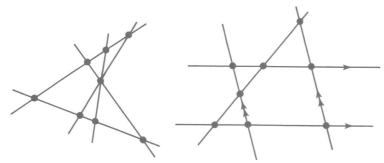

⬛		1		⬛	1		⬛	⬛		1
⬛	3	7		⬛	7	1		⬛	7	3
1	7	⬛		1	1	⬛		1	3	⬛

97 Intersecting lines

5 lines : 8 intersections

One solution to the second problem is to have a set of five parallel lines crossing a set of four parallel lines to give 20 intersections, and the 10th line through one of these points of intersection cutting the other seven lines.

Another neat solution is to have two intersecting pencils of five lines.

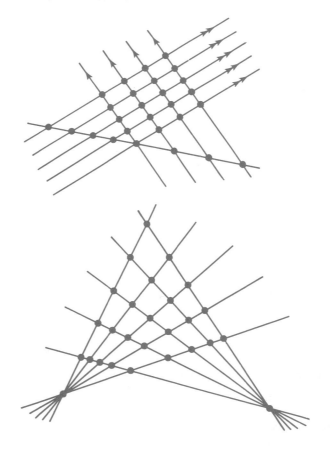

98   One-upmanship!

Yes, she is right. If $n_1, n_2, ..., n_8$ are consecutive numbers then $n_1^2 + n_4^2 + n_6^2 + n_7^2 = n_2^2 + n_3^2 + n_5^2 + n_8^2$ is always true.

Let the first number be n then the others will be $n+1, n+2, ..., n+7$.

Now $n^2 + (n+3)^2 + (n+5)^2 + (n+6)^2 = 4n^2 + 28n + 70$

and $(n+1)^2 + (n+2)^2 + (n+4)^2 + (n+7)^2 = 4n^2 + 28n + 70$

thus proving that Elizabeth was right.

99   The Grand Prix circuit

The difference in distance travelled in going around circles of radii R and r is

$$2\pi R - 2\pi r = 2\pi(R-r)$$

so for the car it would be 4π metres and it would be just the same for one lap of the circuit.

The actual radius of each bend does not matter and most of the right-hand bends are cancelled by left-hand bends, as will always be the case with a simple closed curve.

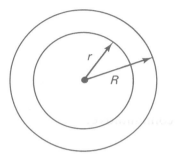

100   Robotics

One solution is r^2tr^3 which means first do operation r three times then operation t then operation r twice, i.e. work from right to left.

$$ABCD \xrightarrow{r} DABC \xrightarrow{r} CDAB \xrightarrow{r} BCDA \xrightarrow{t} CBDA \xrightarrow{r} ACBD \xrightarrow{r} DACB.$$

Alternative solutions also requiring six stages are r^3trt and $trtr^2t$.

It can be achieved with more than six stages but not fewer.

101   Think again!

No amount of differencing or formulae will help solve this one. Each new line counts the digits in the previous line so

    3   1   2   2   1   1

is counted from the left as

    one 3, one 1, two 2s, and two 1s

and replacing the words by digits we have the sequence

    1   3   1   1   2   2   2   1

which is the last line given.

The next line is then

1 1 1 3 2 1 3 2 1 1

and the next

3 1 1 3 1 2 1 1 1 3 1 2 2 1

With a little thought you can see that no digit can occur four times so 4 can never be in the sequence, or any higher digit for that matter.

102 Squared sums!

D. St P. Barnard's puzzles are well worth collecting as many of them are of a mathematical nature. His other solution to a pair of 4-digit numbers was

$$(5288 + 1984)^2 = 52\,881\,984$$

This must be one of the few situations where addition is not commutative!

$$(0 + 1)^2 = 01 \qquad (8 + 1)^2 = 81$$
$$(20 + 25)^2 = 2025$$
$$(30 + 25)^2 = 3025$$
$$(98 + 01)^2 = 9801$$

The obvious question now arises, can we find solutions to

$$(abc + def)^2 = abc\,def$$

Over to you!

103 A doubly magic triangle

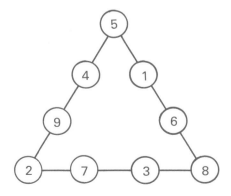

$$5 + 1 + 6 + 8 = 2 + 7 + 3 + 8 = 2 + 9 + 4 + 5 = 20$$
$$5^2 + 1^2 + 6^2 + 8^2 = 2^2 + 7^2 + 3^2 + 8^2 = 2^2 + 9^2 + 4^2 + 5^2 = 126$$

104 The travelling salesman problem

The shortest route for Mrs Lavender is 91 miles which is achieved as follows.

$$Ex \to Oke \to Cred \to Tiv \to Cull \to Ex \to Exm \to Ex$$
$$\quad 23 \quad\; 16 \quad\; 11 \quad\; 8 \quad\; 13 \quad\; 10 \quad\; 10$$

When Honiton is included the shortest route is achieved by taking the same route as before to Cullompton and then to Honiton followed by Exmouth and back to Exeter, giving a total distance of 100 miles.

As the shortest route never crosses itself it is in effect a simple closed curve so it would make no difference which town on it was taken as the base. However, if Mrs Lavender could finish at a different town to her starting point then she would clearly choose Okehampton to end the day, having travelled the route in reverse, thus saving herself 23 miles.

105 Ever more triangles and squares

Two equilateral triangles can be made by having one with an edge length of 3 short straws(ss) and one with an edge length of 1 short straw.

(a) Edge length 4 ss.

(b) One with edge length 2 ss and two with edge length 1 ss.

(c) Four with edge length 1 ss.

(d)  or

(e)  or ... or ...

(f) ... or an octahedron, but see (l).

(g) Edge length 3 ss.

(h) One edge length 2 ss and one edge length 1 ss.

(i) Each edge length 1 ss.

(j)

(k) a cube edge length 1 ss.

(l) An octahedron edge length 1 ss. Each face is an equilateral triangle, each plane of symmetry through four vertices gives a square, see the figure where one of the squares is shaded. Better, make it up by threading shirring elastic through your straws.

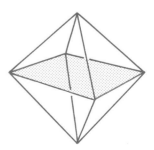

106 Edging along the octahedron

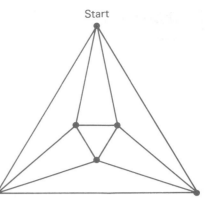

Start

The number of routes from one vertex of an octahedron to visit every edge once and return to the original vertex is 1488.

How many did you find?

It may help you to consider all the routes if you use a topological transformation of the edges of the octahedron such as that shown here.

107 Toilet tissue thickness

Don't be confused by the spiral winding. If the thickness of the tissue is d cm and the length of tissue on the roll is l cm then $l \times d$ is the area of the cross-section of paper on the roll.

Now

$$l = 240 \times 14 = 3360 \, \text{cm}$$

and the area of cross-section is the difference between the areas of circles of diameters 11 cm and 4 cm

$$= \tfrac{\pi}{4}(11^2 - 4^2) \simeq 82.47 \, \text{cm}^2$$

so the thickness of the tissue $\simeq 82.47 \div 3360 \simeq 0.0245 \, \text{cm}$.

The thickness of all the turns of tissue on a full roll is 3.5 cm so the number of turns is $3.5 \div 0.0245 \simeq 143$.

108 Fun with subtraction

When the starting point has the smallest number opposite to the largest number the end point appears to arrive within five stages but if this is avoided longer sequences can be formed with surprisingly small numbers. The solution below was found by a girl in a local middle school.

start	0	2	6	13							
first differences		2	4	7	13						
second differences		2	3	6	11						
third differences			1	3	5	9					
fourth differences			2	2	4	8					
fifth differences				0	2	4	6				
sixth differences				2	2	2	6				
seventh differences					0	0	4	4			
eighth differences					0	4	0	4			
ninth differences						4	4	4	4		

No longer sequence is possible.

110

109 Make a century

$$3 + \frac{69258}{714} \qquad 81 + \frac{5643}{297} \qquad 81 + \frac{7524}{396} \qquad 82 + \frac{3546}{197}$$

$$91 + \frac{5742}{638} \qquad 91 + \frac{5823}{647} \qquad 91 + \frac{7524}{836} \qquad 94 + \frac{1578}{263}$$

$$96 + \frac{1428}{357} \qquad 96 + \frac{1752}{438} \qquad 96 + \frac{2148}{537}$$

110 Know your cube

60° not 90°!

Complete the triangle to see that its sides will all be diagonals of a face of the cube, so the triangle is equilateral.

111 Mixed doubles

The solution is not unique. One solution is as follows

	Court 1	Court 2
Match 1	Aa v Bb	Cc v Dd
Match 2	Ab v Cd	Dc v Ba
Match 3	Ad v Da	Bc v Cb

Note that there are six ways of picking two men from the four available namely AB, AC, AD, BC, BD, CD and similarly six ways of choosing the women ab, ac, ad, bc, bd, cd. The skill now comes in meshing these together to fulfil the given conditions. How many distinct solutions are there?

112 Siting the airport terminal

Interestingly P can be anywhere inside the triangle for the sum of the perpendiculars will be constant.

Consider a limiting case with P on AC. Then

$$\begin{aligned} PN + PL &= x \cos 30° + y \cos 30° \\ &= (x + y) \cos 30° \\ &= d \cos 30° \end{aligned}$$

where d is the length of the side of ABC.

But this length is equal to the perpendicular distance from B to AC, see the dotted line in figure (i).

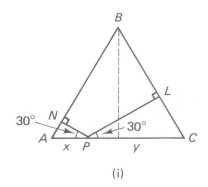

(i)

Now consider the general case, see (ii). Draw a line through P parallel to AC then $PN + PL = BT$ so $PN + PL + PM = BD$, the length of an altitude of $\triangle ABC$.

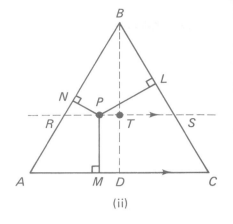

(ii)

113 Reconstructing the manor house

18m by 8m by 4m

If the length, breadth and height of the room are a, b and c feet respectively, then

$$ac = 72 \qquad bc = 32 \qquad ab = 144$$

from which $\qquad c^2 = \dfrac{ac.bc}{ab} = \dfrac{72 \times 32}{144} = 16$

giving $\qquad c = 4$

Then $\qquad a = \dfrac{ac}{c} = \dfrac{72}{4} = 18$

and $\qquad b = \dfrac{bc}{c} = \dfrac{32}{4} = 8$

114 Who came in second?

At first it appears that there is not enough data. But there are 40 points awarded in all, and making the reasonable assumptions that

i) each event is allocated the same number of points
ii) a different positive number of points is allocated to each of the first three positions

then the following scoring systems need to be considered

5 events scoring (4,3,1) or (5,2,1)
4 events scoring (5,3,2) or (6,3,1) or (7,2,1)

Only one of these will satisfy the remaining conditions and leads to

	javelin	event 2	event 3	event 4	event 5	
Tom	2	5	5	5	5	22
Dick	5	1	1	1	1	9
Harry	1	2	2	2	2	9

So Harry was second in all but the javelin.

112

115 Chess board tours

Rook's tours

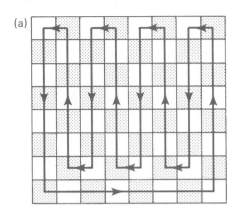

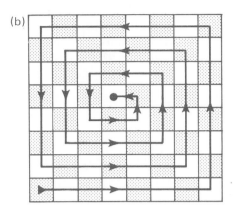

At least 15 changes of direction are required for a re-entrant tour, see (a), whilst the non re-entrant tour can be achieved with 14 changes of direction as in (b).

It is impossible for a rook to make a complete tour of the board from one corner to the opposite corner. To move from bottom left to top right the rook will undergo a displacement of 7 squares to the right and 7 squares up. That is a total of 14 squares. On the tour any further moves to the right must be balanced by equivalent moves to the left, and further moves up must be balanced by equivalent moves down. Thus, to reach the square in the top corner the rook must visit an even number of squares. But to complete the tour it must visit 63 squares. These two requirements are contradictory so the tour is impossible.

On which squares would it be possible for the rook to complete a tour having started at the bottom left hand corner?

Queen's tours

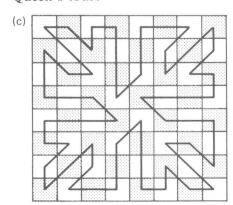

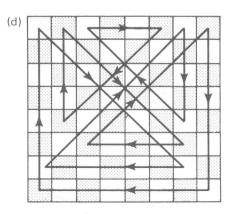

Any tour, achievable by a rook is also possible with a queen so the interest here is with tours which introduce diagonal moves. A very good example of a symmetric re-entrant tour is that of the queen's magic tour. (c) is a re-entrant tour with four-fold rotational symmetry.

(d) is a tour that visits several squares twice but manages to tour the whole board with only thirteen changes of direction.

Bishop's tours

From a black corner square a bishop can only move in one direction so such a square cannot come in the middle of a bishop's tour. It follows that the black corners would then have to be the starting point and end point for any tour which visited all the black squares.

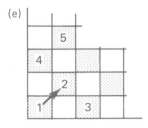

Let such a tour start at the square marked 1 in (e), then as soon as the bishop has moved into square 2 only one of the squares 3 and 4 can be visited. Suppose the bishop moves to square 3, then a little thought shows that square 4 should only be reached as a last move, because there would be only one way of approaching it, that is via square 5. But we have already argued that the end point is at the far corner. Thus a complete tour is not possible.

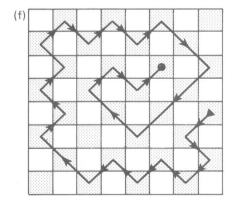

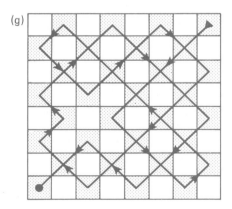

The best that can be achieved by a bishop's tour when squares cannot be revisited is 29 black squares. No matter what you do there will always be at least three black squares which are unattainable. One solution is shown in (f). The most efficient way of visiting all the black squares is shown in (g).

114

116 Amaze your friends

$a + a^* = 728461 + 271538 = 999999$
$c + c^* = 854750 + 145249 = 999999$
i.e. a^* and c^* are the 9's complements of a and c

Now $\qquad 999999 = 1000000 - 1$
So $\qquad$ total $= a + b + a^* + c + c^*$
$\qquad\qquad\qquad = (a + a^*) + (c + c^*) + b$
$\qquad\qquad\qquad = 2000000 - 2 + b$

It follows that the sum of the 5 numbers is obtained by starting with the number b, taking away 2 from its units digit and sticking a 2 at the front.

117 Court card capers

One solution is

Ah	Kc	Qd	Js
Qs	Jd	Ac	Kh
Jc	Qh	Ks	Ad
Kd	As	Jh	Qc

which satisfies all the requirements.

This puzzle is of very long standing for it has existed in a published form from early in the eighteenth century. Euler, the celebrated mathematician, proposed a similar puzzle concerning 36 army officers, six from each of six regiments. But this was later shown to be insoluble. However, should you wish to try another problem of this type which has a solution consider the following.

In a saloon car race there were five teams A, B, C, D and E each with five cars labelled 1, 2, 3, 4 and 5. The starting grid had five rows and the cars were five abreast in a 5 × 5 array. To make the start as fair to each team as possible it was arranged that in any row, or column, or diagonal of the starting grid there would be only one car from each team, and only one car with each number. Find a suitable starting position for the cars.

118 Crossing the desert

By making supply dumps at suitable intervals it is possible for the students to safely travel $416\frac{2}{3}$ miles into the desert.

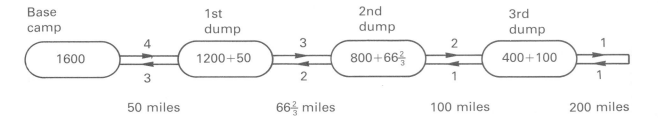

The first supply dump is made at 50 miles from base camp by making 4 outward journeys and 3 return journeys which enables 1250 miles worth of provisions to be established there. This allows '1200 miles' for further progress into the desert plus '50 miles' for the final return to base. The second dump is then made $66\frac{2}{3}$ miles from the first dump by making 3 outward jouneys and 2 return journeys which enables $866\frac{2}{3}$ miles worth of provisions to be established. This allows for '800 miles' further progress plus $66\frac{2}{3}$ to return to the first dump. The third dump is then made at 100 miles from the second dump by making 2 outward journeys and 1 return journey which enables 500 miles worth of provisions to be established there. This allows a further out and back journey of 200 miles and leaves 100 miles worth for the homeward journey to the second dump.

The distance into the desert is then

$$50 + 66\tfrac{2}{3} + 100 + 200 = 416\tfrac{2}{3}$$

but more interestingly it can be expressed as

$$200 \left(\tfrac{1}{4} + \tfrac{1}{3} + \tfrac{1}{2} + 1\right)$$

which gives more insight into the problem.

119 Don't be square

There are 50 possible squares to be found. How many did you miss!

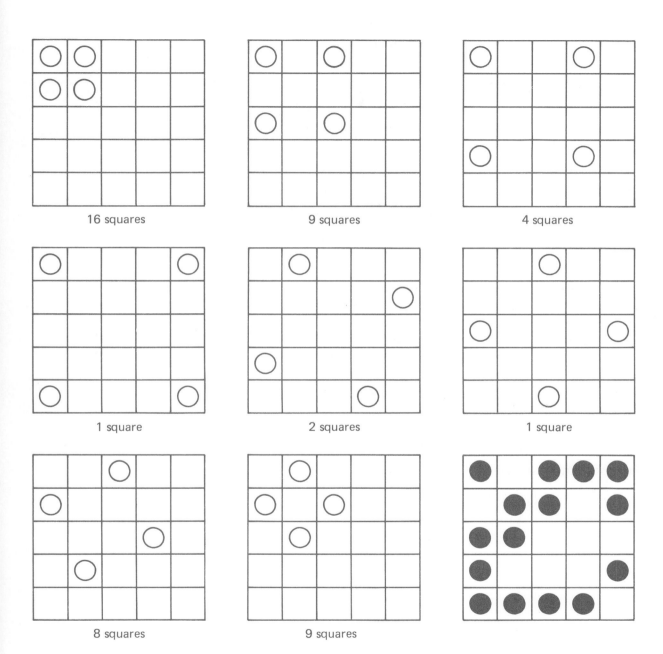

16 squares

9 squares

4 squares

1 square

2 squares

1 square

8 squares

9 squares

It is possible to put fifteen counters on the board so that no four lie at the vertices of a square. One solution is shown here, but it is not unique.

120 Can you help the motorway designer?

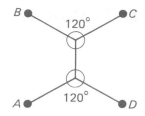

Interestingly the shortest route is as shown, where the motorway has two 3-way junctions, and the roads all meet at 120°. Simple trigonometry shows that the length of this motorway would be 54.6 miles. This solution can be strikingly shown using a soap film stretched between four pins at the vertices of a square between two perspex plates. The solutions of other similar shortest route problems can be demonstrated in this way and often have very surprising solutions. An analysis of these problems, often called Steiner problems after the German mathematician who drew attention to them, is to be found in the book *What is Mathematics?* by Courant and Robbins.

121 Look before you leap!

It is easy to get caught by these and similar questions if you haven't met them before.

1   They both weigh 50 kilograms
2   A hole contains no earth.
3   The ship rises with the tide so the mayoress was faced with 12 rungs to climb.
4   80 p not £1.60
5   One rabbit, the dead one.

122 What's wrong?

This 'proof' that $2 = 1$ can fool many people. The flaw lies in division by $(x - y)$ which is zero disguised. This and many other algebraic fallacies are discussed by Northrop in the chapter aptly called 'Thou shalt not divide by zero' of his book *Riddles in Mathematics*.

123 Calendar capers

When the total was 57 the dates are

$$\frac{57}{3} = 19 \qquad 19 - 7 = 12 \qquad 19 + 7 = 26$$

If the centre number in a column of five dates is D then the five dates are

$$D - 14, \quad D - 7, \quad D, \quad D + 7, \quad D + 14$$

so their total is $5D$. It is thus an easy matter to divide a given total by 5 and add and subtract 7s. When the total is 85 then $D = 17$ so the total corresponds to the last column on the page of the calendar.

If a column started with 6 then the fifth number would be $6 + 7 + 7 + 7 = 34$, but no month has 34 days.

If the first number in a column of four dates is F then the dates are

$$F, \quad F + 7, \quad F + 14, \quad F + 21$$

so their total is

$$T = 4F + 42.$$

Thus to find the dates from the total first subtract 42 and then divide by 4 to find F, before repeatedly adding on 7 to give the other numbers.

$$T \rightarrow \boxed{-42} \rightarrow \boxed{\div 4} \rightarrow F$$

Other interesting patterns occur when looking at sets of numbers placed symmetrically about a centre number such as a cross or H formation.

Their respective totals are $5C$ and $7C$ which makes it very easy to work out C given the total and then to deduce the other numbers.

124 Optimising

If 'positive numbers' are interpreted as whole numbers then the best solution is given by

$$17 = 3 + 3 + 3 + 3 + 3 + 2$$

where the product is $3^5 \times 2 = 486$

But the question should not limit you to whole numbers, and the best solution is given by

$$17 = \frac{17}{6} + \frac{17}{6} + \frac{17}{6} + \frac{17}{6} + \frac{17}{6} + \frac{17}{6}$$

when the product is $(\frac{17}{6})^6 \simeq 517$

See what happens when other numbers are used as a starting point.

125 How not to cancel

$$\frac{1\cancel{6}}{\cancel{6}4} = \frac{1}{4} \qquad \frac{1\cancel{9}}{\cancel{9}5} = \frac{1}{5} \qquad \frac{4\cancel{9}}{\cancel{9}8} = \frac{4}{8}$$

126 Integers only

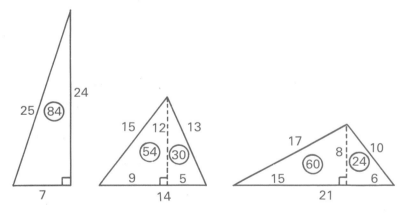

The first triangle is right-angled and the others can be found by first making a collection of right-angled triangles with integer sides and fitting them together where their sides match.

Note, any triangle with sides of length

$$m^2 - n^2, \ 2mn \ \text{and} \ m^2 + n^2$$

where m and n are integers such that m > n will be right-angled.

127 Box designing

Cut the cross along the lines indicated in bold. Then fold A onto B along the line shown dotted. A and B stuck together form the central partition of the box and allow two lids to be hinged at this point. Cut the net out and fold it up to convince yourself that it works.

The trick in designing a net for this box is to solve the problem of the two lids being hinged at the same point; once this has been done finding a net is not difficult, but most solutions will not be as satisfying as the one given.

cut →

| LID | A ┊ B | LID |

← cut

128 A multitude of magic squares

There are 57 distinct solutions not counting reflections and rotations. To find them all a systematic search is required. Consider, for example, the possible solutions with 5 in the centre and hence a magic sum of 15.

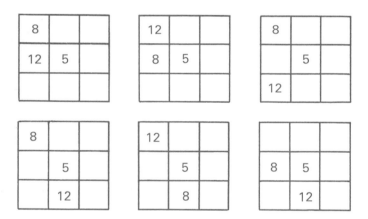

There are 6 different solutions of this kind which can easily be found by filling in the remaining cells using the fact that the row, column and diagonal totals must all be 15. Putting 8 or 12 in the centre leads to 12 more similar solutions.

It is interesting to note that no solution is possible with 5, 8 and 12 in a straight line through the centre, for $5 + 8 + 12 = 25$ which is not 3 times 5, 8 or 12. Three solutions are possible however with 5, 8 and 12 along the first row and $8\frac{1}{3}$ $(= 25 \div 3)$ in the centre.

5	8	12
$15\frac{1}{3}$	$8\frac{1}{3}$	$1\frac{1}{3}$
$4\frac{2}{3}$	$8\frac{2}{3}$	$11\frac{2}{3}$

12	5	8
$4\frac{1}{3}$	$8\frac{1}{3}$	$12\frac{1}{3}$
$8\frac{2}{3}$	$11\frac{2}{3}$	$4\frac{2}{3}$

8	12	5
$5\frac{1}{3}$	$8\frac{1}{3}$	$11\frac{1}{3}$
$11\frac{2}{3}$	$4\frac{2}{3}$	$8\frac{2}{3}$

A summary of the solutions is given in the following table which shows the possible magic totals and the number of solutions with each total.

Magic total	3	9	$13\frac{1}{2}$	15	$19\frac{1}{2}$	21	$22\frac{1}{2}$	24	$24\frac{3}{4}$	25
Number of solutions	3	1	1	6	6	1	1	6	1	3

Magic total	$25\frac{1}{2}$	27	$27\frac{3}{4}$	30	$31\frac{1}{2}$	$34\frac{1}{2}$	36	$40\frac{1}{2}$	45
Number of solutions	6	3	1	6	1	1	6	1	3